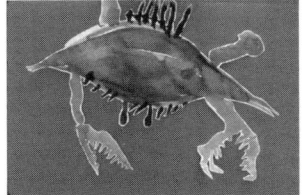

Singing *the* Chesapeake

Featuring Songs by
TOM WISNER

For children of all ages

with additional songs by
Teresa Whitaker and Mark Wisner

Edited by: Teresa Whitaker, Michael Glaser,
Kathleen Glaser, and Frank Schwartz
CD mixing and mastering: Jim Fox
Cover design by Katie Giganti, and a compilation of childrens' art work
All drawings and photos by Tom Wisner, unless specified
Back cover photo by Dave Harp

Made possible by CHESTORY/CHEARS and Finding Home Productions

an O.Ruby Production

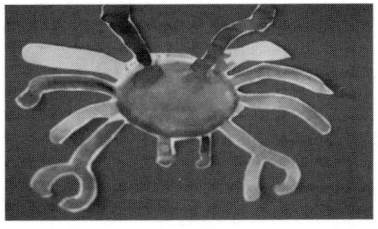

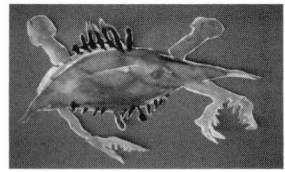

Dedicated to the songs of waters all over the world. May we learn to listen and hear, cherish and share them with our children. And to the voices of children, may the songs you sing give you strength, hope and joy.

Introduction

" **S**unshine over a deep blue sea...A turtle called Susquehanna...I'm made of water, flowing water...Chesapeake Born..."

This collection of songs by Tom Wisner, the "Bard of the Chesapeake," are the living, streaming echoes of a unique, lifelong dedication and creative act of service—Tom's deep commitment to environmental education and awareness that he shared through music.

Like all great artists, Tom was drawn to a few central themes: the natural wonder of the Chesapeake Bay, the mystery of our own unity within the life web of nature, the flowing water of generations, and our vital connections with the natural world.

A man of enormous artistic integrity and awareness, Tom heard music in every breath and movement of nature, in every feather, stone, and leaf, in the softness of water's touch, in the flight of the great blue heron…in the soaring fish hawk's wing.

Tom's calling was elemental. His commitment was to awaken a deeper awareness of our personal responsibility to the common good of all living beings and living systems of our Earth. He left every audience with a heightened personal consciousness of their awesome power to continue, or not, the life-giving story of the Chesapeake Bay.

When he worked with children he always began from a place of connection, engaging their imaginations and instilling awe and wonder. As he said, "I want to move children's hearts to learn…that they are participants in the mystery of creation…and the health of the Bay. I want them to make the Bay a friend for life!"

About his own songs he said, "My songs are the result of a lifetime of thinking and teaching about a relationship to this land and its waters. Singing together creates a living, vital sense of community. My songs are celebrations encouraging all to join!"

It is our hope that singing and sharing these songs, especially with children, will deepen everyone's connection to Chesapeake life, ways, and rhythms, and will be indeed…a celebration!

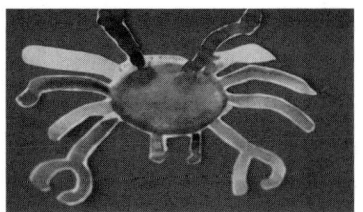

Gratitude and thanks to the circle and community of many, whose friendship, care and creativity infuse this work. Special thanks to Joan Clement (CHESTORY/CHEARS) and to the Calvert Marine Museum, Jim Fox, Sara Leeland, Mary Ellen and Walter Boynton (see Acknowledgements page 55).

Over the years, Tom worked with many different educators. Betty Brady, a gifted, insightful and energetic 5th grade teacher at Hollywood Elementary School in St. Mary's County, welcomed Tom to her classroom many times. The following are her recollections:

"Tom Wisner used the power of fun to educate us. For decades he demonstrated that schoolwork can be fun, that the arts can be naturally and effectively woven back into curricular content, inviting receptivity and interactive learning. He included singing, dancing, drawing and painting, composing, writing, sculpting, and performing. These songs are a place to begin. They give us joy and unity so that we sing them again and again, sooner or later internalizing what we sing. Saying the words gives a joyous renewal to an awareness of our innate connections to Earth, an affirmation of our oneness with nature.

Tom's wisdom was reuniting the arts with the earth sciences. Doing that is a gift, especially for the lives that children lead in classrooms. In joy and fun, learning is natural and simple, deep, effective and contagious. The creative arts have the power to level our differences. They provide a common emotive language where continuing dialogue with self and others helps extrapolate significant meanings. This music, these words, are just a beginning. Follow them…through all the art forms."

Table of Contents

* To hear these tracks go to Smithsonian Folkways and find the CD, *We've Got to Come Full Circle* by Tom Wisner.

"If a child can be taught to view the earth as a scientist does, then why not as an artist does?"

Tom Wisner: *"The experience of connection is the essence of teaching about the Bay, and connection comes through contact. Learning is about putting yourself into relation with all things of nature that pique your interest and listening with all senses alive within and without: with imagery, with touch, with emotion and with thought—all awakening to the great silence.*

When kids are young and in love with the earth and its animals—the arts can help children express their love for the earth—help them to project themselves into the life of another creature and have true empathy for another part of creation. The arts do that better than any other form of education.

To draw and sing the blue crab—is to become the blue crab.

Children need to see someone model that kind of deep involvement. Children need to engage deeply with the natural world and its creatures, beginning with their own 'home place.' And then they need to engage in art-making to express their experiences of those connections.

I tell them, 'Become the thing you love!'"

Made of Water

"Each day the sun picks up water out of the ocean and carries it over the 64,000 square land miles of the Chesapeake Basin to drop again and flow down to make rivers and the Chesapeake Bay. If you live anywhere in that 64,000-mile drainage basin then you're reborn every day into the waters of the Chesapeake. You and I are made of nearly 90% water, so if you live here in the basin, then you're made of these waters and you are Chesapeake born with the cycle of those waters. You're made of the water, and you're part of these rivers and this water cycle."

—Tom Wisner

SONGS

Made of Water • A song celebrating that indeed we are "made of water." Tom often used gestures (hand and whole body) to show key lyrics. He borrowed from Native American signs as well as American Sign Language. Gestures can also be created by reading the lyrics out loud and asking children how they would show those words. The gestures can be expanded into whole body movements like a dance.

Dribus Go the Rain • This fanciful song describes the water cycle. Some of the language is a "made up" language playing with the rhythms of syllables and consonants.

Prettiest Marsh • Marshes are vital to the health of the Bay and all waterways. Each one is a whole other world unto itself. Brimming with life, colors, sounds and smells, they are also mysterious and reflective places. Quiet focused times of listening in an actual site are a component of immersion education. Marshes provide rich opportunities to isolate senses and to experience nature in deep and surprising new ways.

Sunshine Bankers • *"There is a flow of life from air (oxygen) to water and the sun to the Bay to grow grasses and phytoplankton…zooplankton (pronounced 'zo' like 'oh!')… larger shrimp…fish…you! The sun! And all its wonderful life power, penetrating as deep as silts will allow, touching the small plant creatures with life so they can be gobbled by small creatures that go off to grace the tables of even larger critters. And the gobbling goes on! Each life becomes more life!"*

Sunshine • *"It's the sun, the wonderful, warm, gracious, generous sun that's behind it all."* This song also celebrates the rhythms of day and night; the dance of moon and sun.

Please note: The tracks on the CD accompanying this songbook cover many years of Tom's singing these songs. Some are early versions and some are older versions. You may notice differences between lyrics and tempos reflected in the charts and what you will hear on the CD. True to the "folk process," Tom was always changing the ways he sang his songs. Listeners are encouraged to do the same—create your own versions that "sing" truest for you.

Made of Water

Words and Music by
TOM WISNER

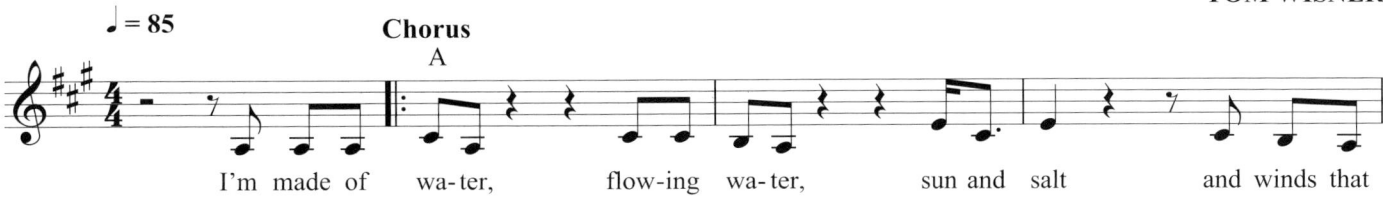

Chorus

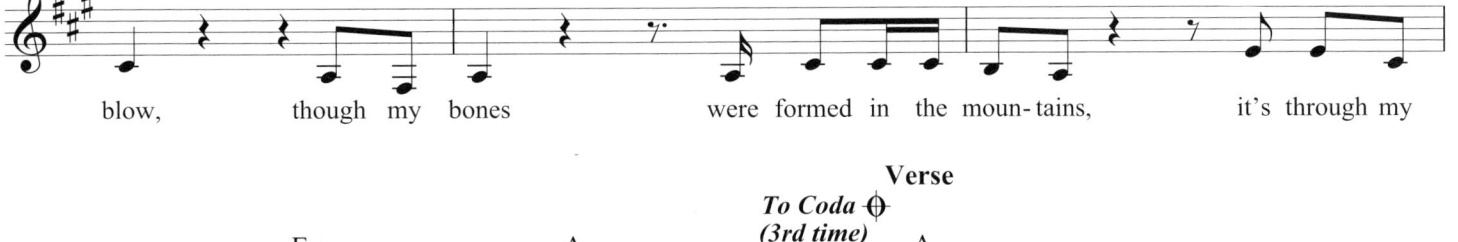

I'm made of wa-ter, flow-ing wa-ter, sun and salt and winds that

blow, though my bones were formed in the moun-tains, it's through my

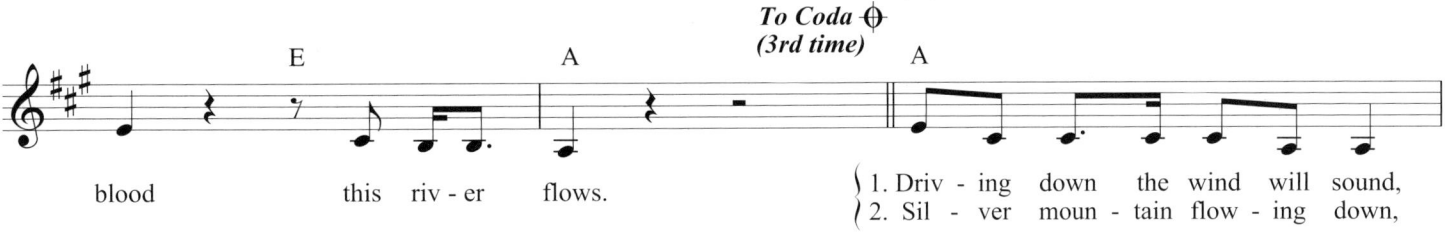

Verse

To Coda ⊕
(3rd time)

blood this riv-er flows.

1. Driv-ing down the wind will sound,
2. Sil-ver moun-tain flow-ing down,

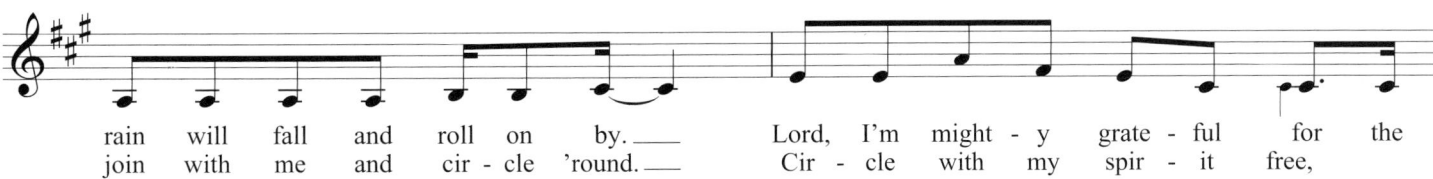

rain will fall and roll on by. ____ Lord, I'm might-y grate-ful for the
join with me and cir-cle 'round. ____ Cir-cle with my spir-it free,

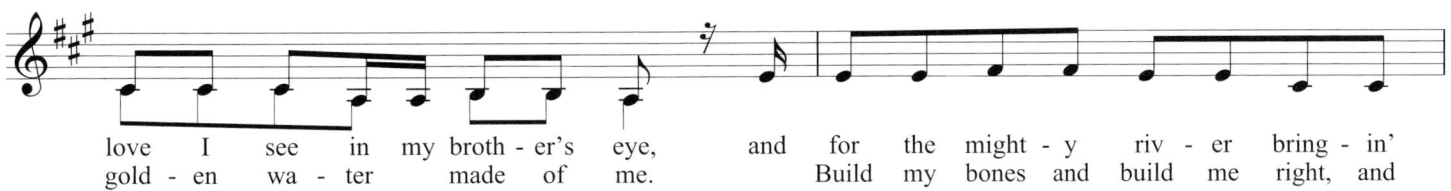

love I see in my broth-er's eye, and for the might-y riv-er bring-in'
gold-en wa-ter made of me. Build my bones and build me right, and

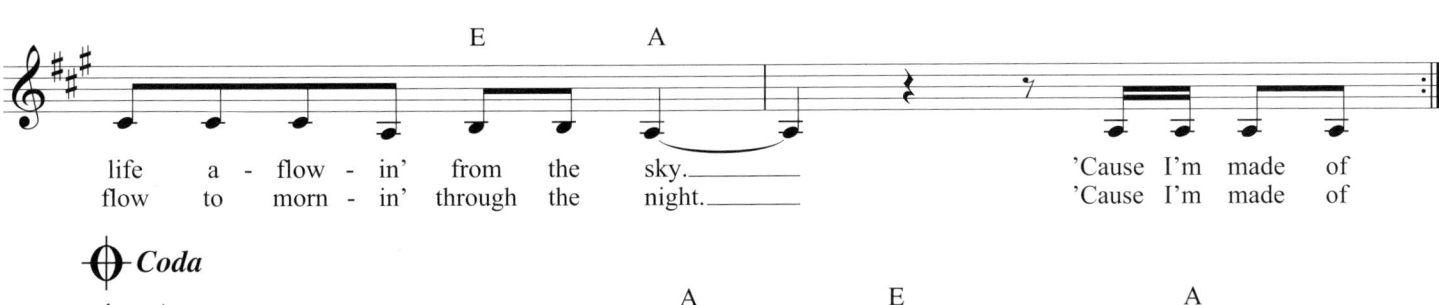

life a-flow-in' from the sky. ____ 'Cause I'm made of
flow to morn-in' through the night. ____ 'Cause I'm made of

⊕ *Coda*

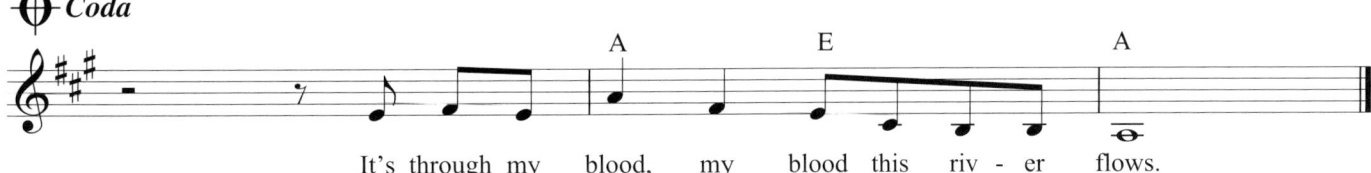

It's through my blood, my blood this riv-er flows.

7

Dribus Go the Rain

Words and Music by
TOM WISNER

gol - ly, sun will melt the shad - ows, and drib - us go the rain.

Haul a gus - ta wind, will blow. Roll a bust - a wave will

go. Sun will melt the shad - ows and drib - us go the rain.

Haul a gus - ta wind will blow. Roll a bust - a wave will

go. Sun will melt the shad - ows, and dri - bus go the rain.

2. *See additional lyrics* rain, (drib - us go the rain), drib - us go the

rain, (drib - us go the rain), drib - us go the rain, (drib - us go the rain).

Additional Lyrics

2. Magic in the drops of ocean lifting,
Joining with the winds and clouds a drifting.
Journey through the seasons and travel cross the land.
Fall to form the streams that join together,
reach to touch the life down by the sea.
I am mostly made of water and this
old river flows through me.

Prettiest Marsh

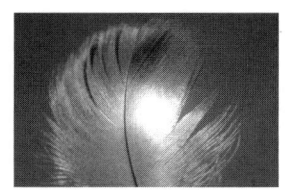

Words and Music by
TERESA WHITAKER

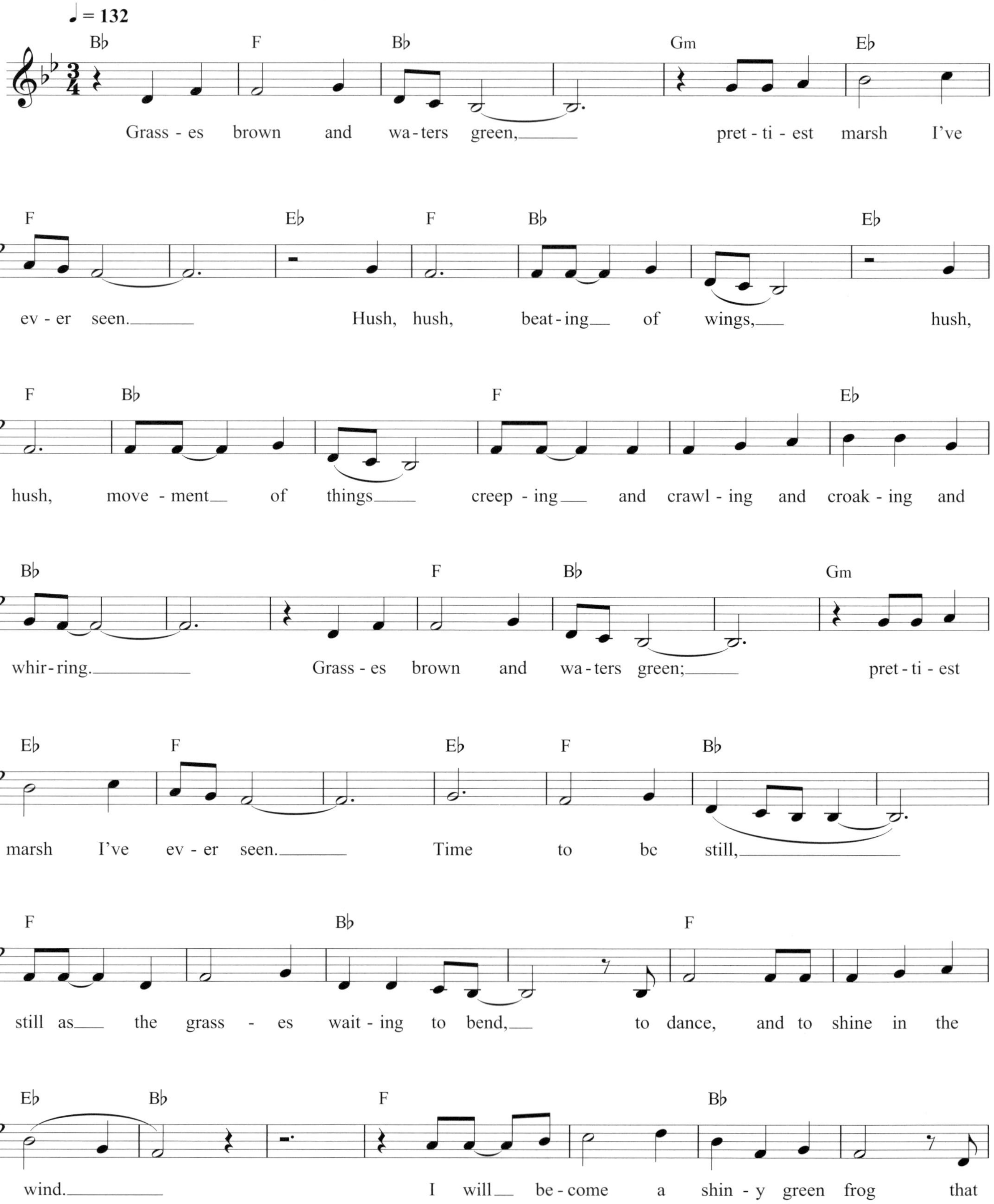

♩ = 132
B♭ F B♭ Gm E♭
Grass - es brown and wa - ters green, pret - ti - est marsh I've
F E♭ F B♭ E♭
ev - er seen. Hush, hush, beat - ing of wings, hush,
F B♭ F E♭
hush, move - ment of things creep - ing and crawl - ing and croak - ing and
B♭ F B♭ Gm
whir - ring. Grass - es brown and wa - ters green; pret - ti - est
E♭ F E♭ F B♭
marsh I've ev - er seen. Time to bc still,
F B♭ F
still as the grass - es wait - ing to bend, to dance, and to shine in the
E♭ B♭ F B♭
wind. I will be - come a shin - y green frog that

Sunshine Bankers

Traditional Melody
Words by TOM WISNER

*Note: This song can be performed as
a round – one meaure between voices.*

Moderately ♩ = 160

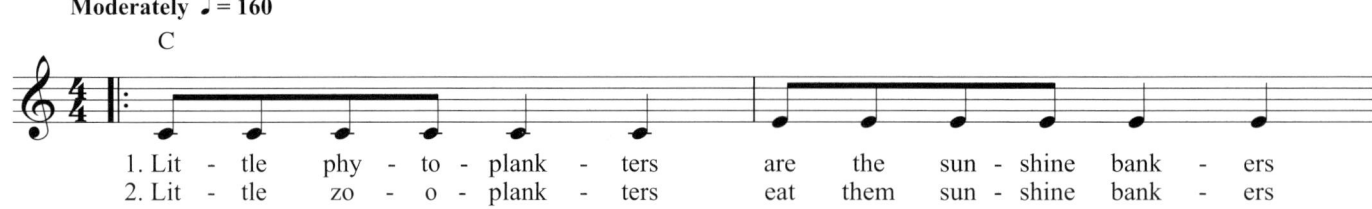

1. Lit - tle phy - to - plank - ters   are   the   sun - shine   bank - ers
2. Lit - tle   zo - o - plank - ters   eat   them   sun - shine   bank - ers

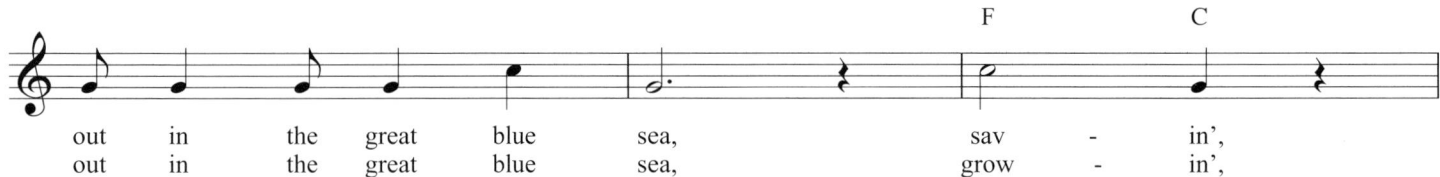

out   in   the   great   blue   sea,   sav - in',
out   in   the   great   blue   sea,   grow - in',

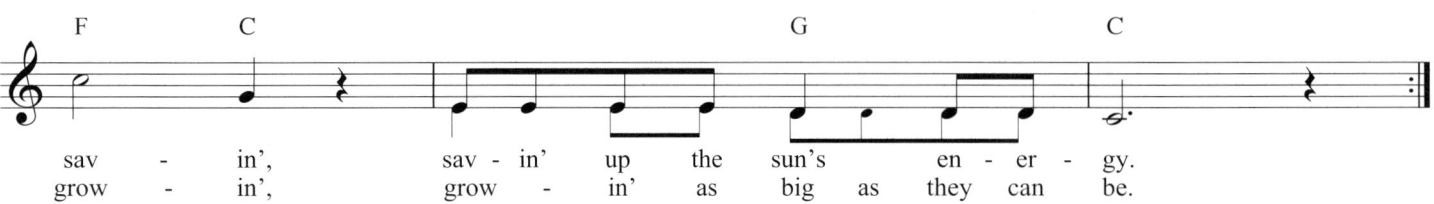

sav - in',   sav - in'   up   the   sun's   en - er - gy.
grow - in',   grow - in'   as   big   as   they   can   be.

3. Oys - ters   on   the   bot - tom   take   in   wa - ter   and   they   got   'em
4. Fish   are   cra - zy   prank - sters,   they   eat   those   zo - o - plank - ters

out   in   the   great   blue   sea,   grow - in',
out   in   the   great   blue   sea,   grow - in',

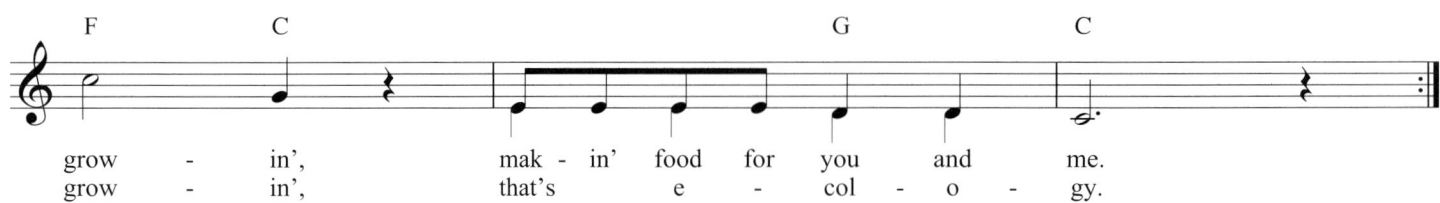

grow - in',   mak - in'   food   for   you   and   me.
grow - in',   that's   e - col - o - gy.

"You can sit down together

in the dark before the dawn

awaiting the song sung, to remake the sun.

Hear your voices rise singing

invoking life ringing

and you and the song

and the sun become one."

"What a gift! And a gift it is!
Life! Living things fill me with joy.
The more to see, the more joy to know."

"Take your breath into your body
Give yourself up to the wind
Let the laughter of the sun
Warm your bones again.
May the waters rise within you
Lift your heart up to your goal
May you walk within the mother
In rhythm with her soul."

— (Tom Wisner songs and poems)

Sunshine

Words by Music by
TOM WISNER

14

Talked to the Heron

"Empathy is an essential part of learning to care for the wild beings of our planet. ...One of the best ways to become aware of our deep connections to all of life is found in the art of personification. I imagine, I am a fish or I am a river and then I speak as that.

*We need to express our connections and to look at the Bay as a mysterious body that we must learn to **relate** to...instead of **use**."*

—Tom Wisner

SONGS

These songs invite using imagination to project into the life experience of another creature.

How Does It Feel To Be A Fish? • Use lots of hand movements and "fish face" expressions when singing this song.

Crabs • A song describing crabs' amazing abilities as well as their delectability.

Geese Come Down • *"Paying attention to the symbol of migrating waterfowl, fish and other wildlife reminds us of how the Chesapeake community of life reaches out over the continent. Caring for the life of our region is an important cog in caring for the life of the continent."*

Dance Sideways • *"The two front claws of a crab are like our arms and legs; they bend and they also rotate. Their two swim fins on the rear are the same. These four limbs have lots of action and ability. Their other six legs bend like our elbows, but they don't rotate. This enables them to shuffle (quickly) to the right or left...causing them to 'dance sideways!'"*

Talked To The Heron • Sing standing up. Have FUN!

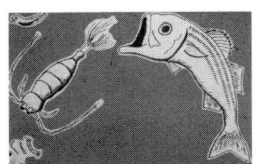

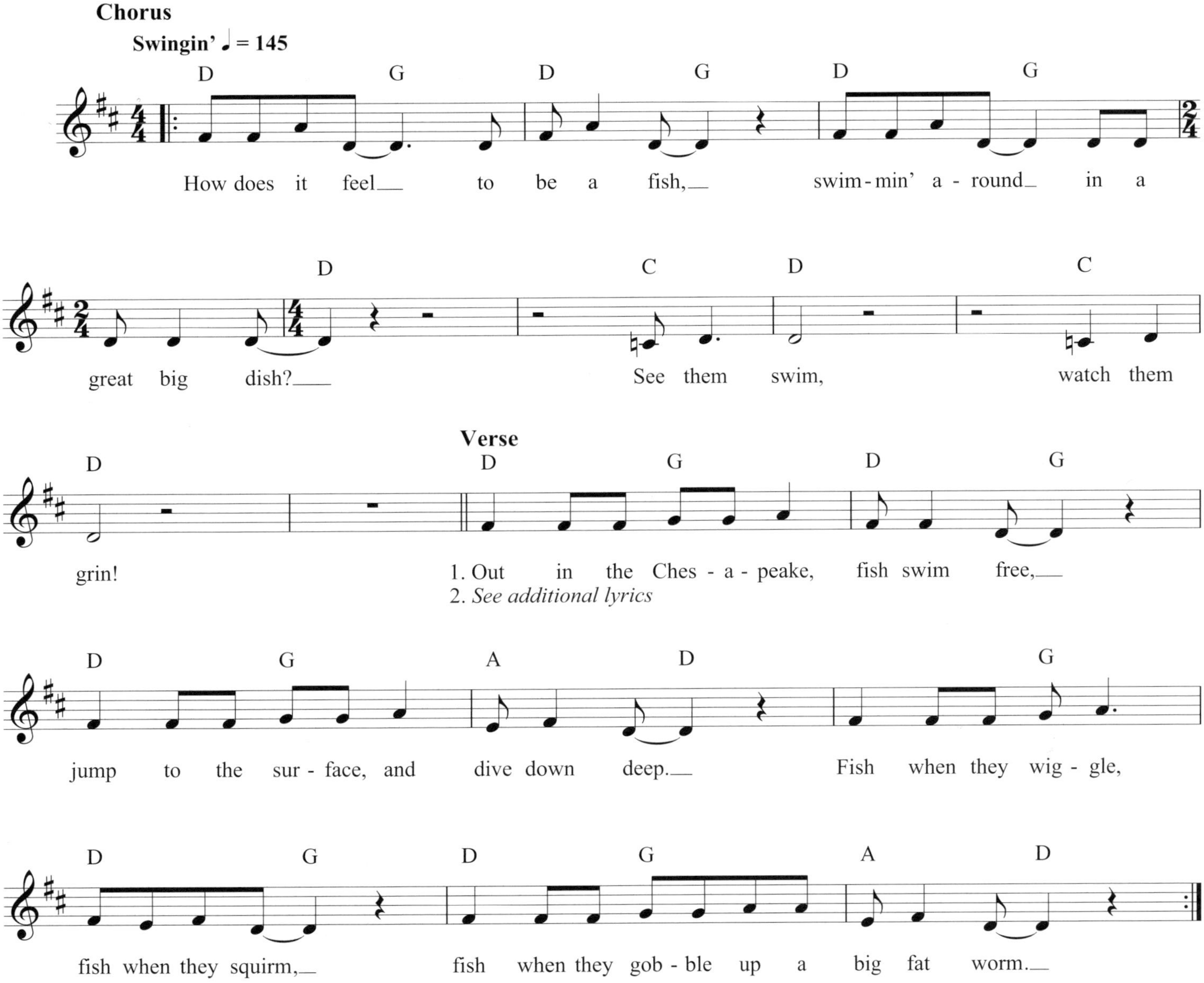

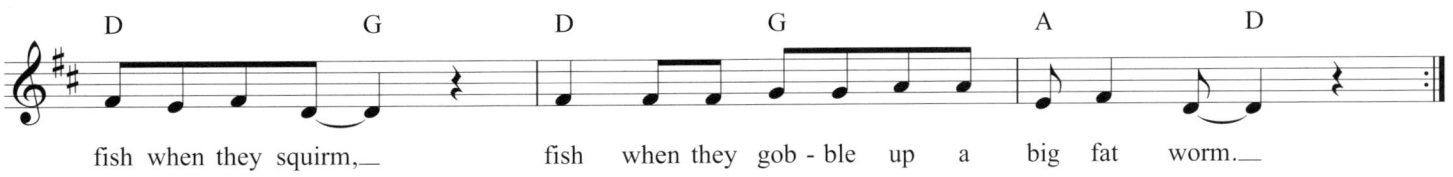

How Does It Feel to Be a Fish?

Words and Music by
TERESA WHITAKER

Chorus
Swingin' ♩ = 145
D G D G D G
How does it feel to be a fish, swim-min' a-round in a
D C D C
great big dish? See them swim, watch them
D
grin!
Verse
D G D G
1. Out in the Ches-a-peake, fish swim free,
2. See additional lyrics
D G A D G
jump to the sur-face, and dive down deep. Fish when they wig-gle,
D G D G A D
fish when they squirm, fish when they gob-ble up a big fat worm.

Additional Lyrics

2. Some fish look happy, some look mean.
   Some look like people that I've seen;
   fishes with glasses, fishes with hats,
   fishes with whiskers just like a cat's.
   Chorus

3. Get you a net and wade in the water,
   if you do it right you ought-a catch a lotta.
   Fish of different colors, fishes so neat,
   fish of different sizes, fishes good to eat.
   Chorus

Crabs

Words and Music by
JIM RASIN and TOM WISNER

Verse

♩ = 120

1. Crabs live in the Ches - a - peake Bay, and oth - er plac - es
2. *(See additional lyrics)*

too.   We are glad this ver - y great day to show a crab to

Chorus

you.   Watch him eat, can you see___ what he's do - in'?

Watch his mouth, count the parts___ that are mov - in'.   Watch him swim,

watch him walk,   what would he say if he could talk?

Additional Lyrics

2. Crabs are good in nature's plan,
   but always wear a frown.
   They eat trash and so they help man,
   to keep pollution down.
   Chorus

3. Crabs are mean and angry guys,
   so keep your hands well back.
   If you see him looking cross-eyed,
   he'll probably attack!
   Chorus

4. Crabs are neat to watch real close
   with all their different feet.
   All my friends are ready to boast
   that crabs are good to eat.
   Chorus

"I believe art is our principle way of connecting with different life forms. Art is a way of learning about the voice of nature.

The arts can also carry the revelations and complexities of science to children. One way of connecting science and art is through 'naming.' Kids would say, 'What's that?' And I would ask them, 'What would you call it?' So they'd look really closely and they'd name a blue crab, 'Ten legged paddle swimmer,' or a Nereid worm, 'Many foot worm.'"

—Tom Wisner

Draw them! Paint them!
Mold them in clay!

Try to show their many parts,
Their actions!
Their beauty!

Tom engaged childrens' imaginations through what he called "hands-on," "hearts-on," "minds-on," "eyes-on" ways of learning. Direct contact with Chesapeake creatures and waters was essential and so were the arts. He used painting, photography, collage-making, modeling with clay, dancing, role-playing, puppetry, poetry, storytelling and lots of singing.

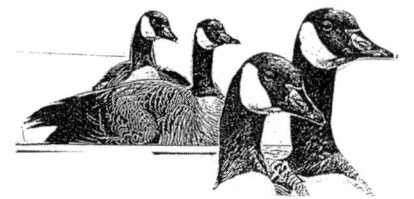

Geese Come Down

Words and Music by
TERESA WHITAKER

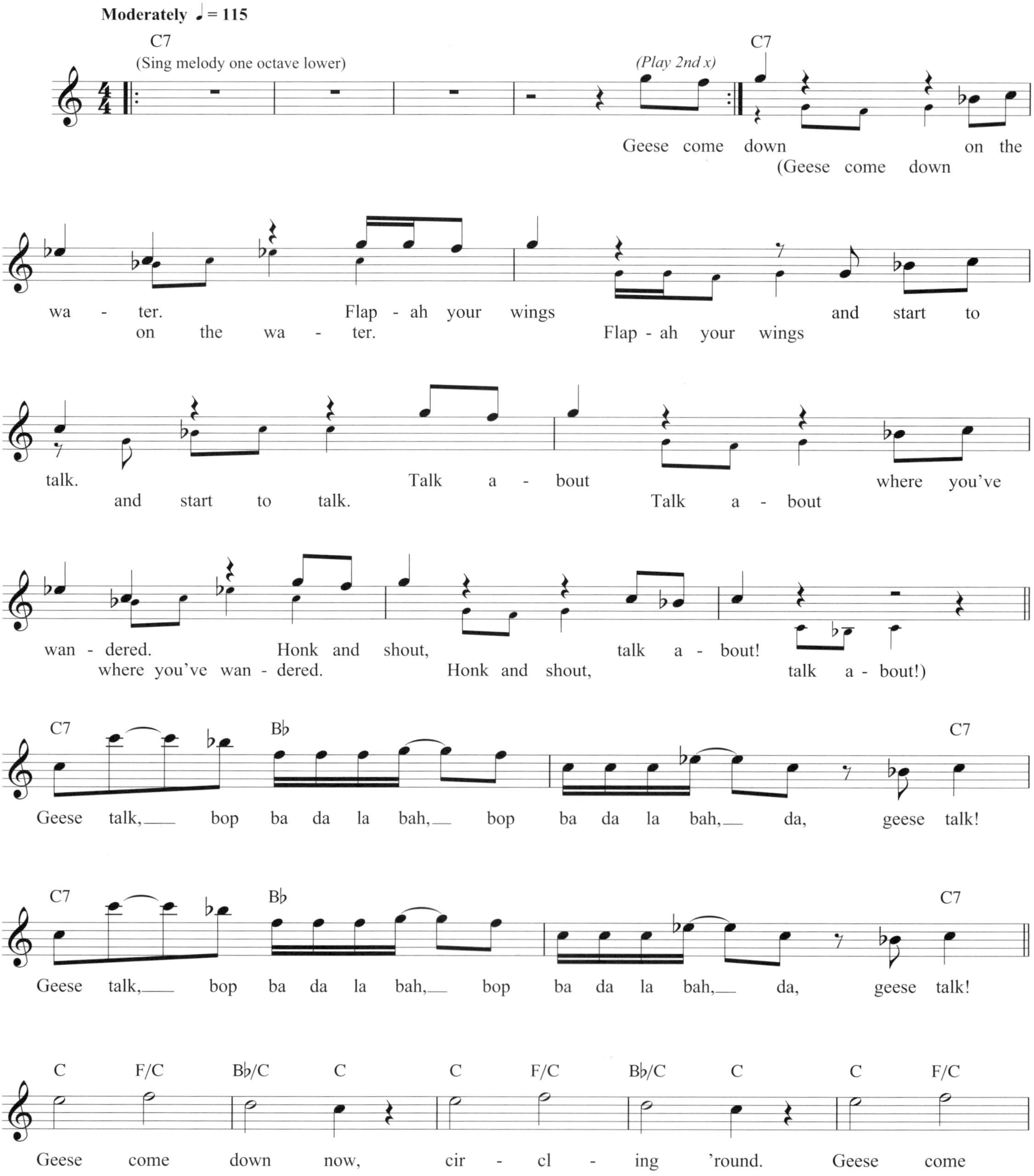

Moderately ♩ = 115
C7
(Sing melody one octave lower)
(Play 2nd x)
C7
Geese come down on the wa - ter. Flap - ah your wings and start to talk. Talk a - bout where you've wan - dered. Honk and shout, talk a - bout!
(Geese come down on the wa - ter. Flap - ah your wings and start to talk. Talk a - bout where you've wan - dered. Honk and shout, talk a - bout!)
C7 Bb C7
Geese talk, bop ba da la bah, bop ba da la bah, da, geese talk!
C7 Bb C7
Geese talk, bop ba da la bah, bop ba da la bah, da, geese talk!
C F/C Bb/C C C F/C Bb/C C C F/C
Geese come down now, cir - cl - ing 'round. Geese come

Dance Sideways

**Words and Music by
TOM WISNER**

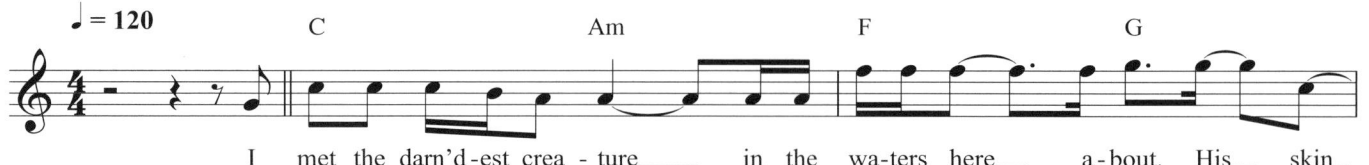

I met the darn'd-est crea-ture____ in the wa-ters here____ a-bout. His____ skin

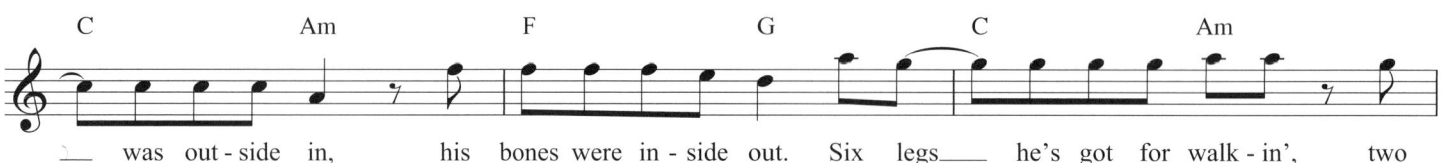

____ was out-side in, his bones were in-side out. Six legs____ he's got for walk-in', two

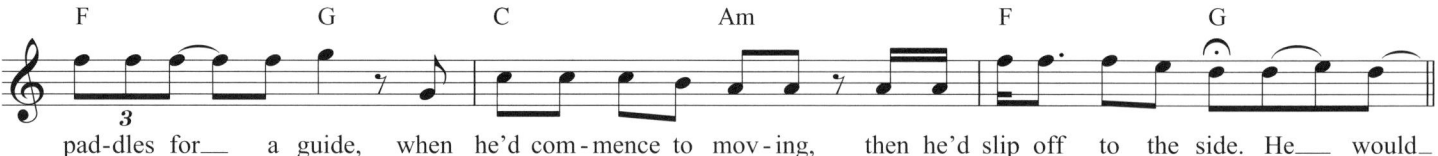

pad-dles for____ a guide, when he'd com-mence to mov-ing, then he'd slip off to the side. He____ would____

____ dance____ side-ways,____ to get where he____ was go-ing, he____ would dance side-

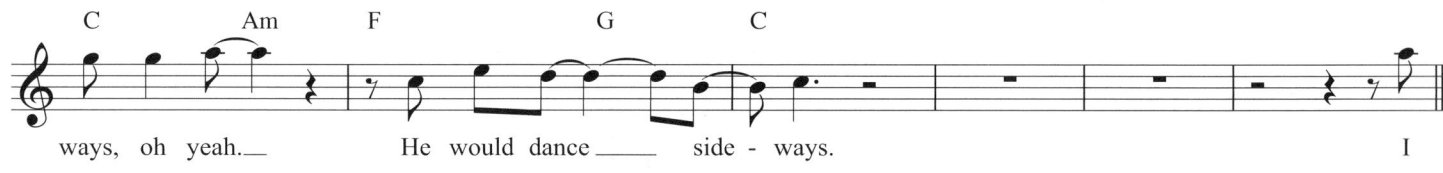

ways, oh yeah.____ He would dance____ side-ways. I

won-der if some peo-ple ev-er won-der what it's like to be put in-to____ a ket-tle and

have a lid snapped tight.____ You wan-der in the dark-ness you can't find your way a-round, des-

Talked to the Heron

Words by TOM WISNER
Adapted to Traditional Melody

Well, you talked to the her-on, and the her-on said, "You

got to get the rhy-thm of the head, ding, dong, you got to get the rhy-thm of the

head, ding, dong." You talked to the her-on, and the her-on said, "You

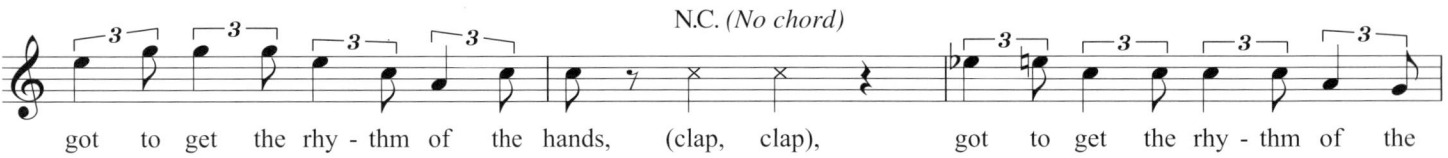

got to get the rhy-thm of the hands, (clap, clap), got to get the rhy-thm of the

hands, (clap, clap)." Talked to the her-on, and the her-on said, "You

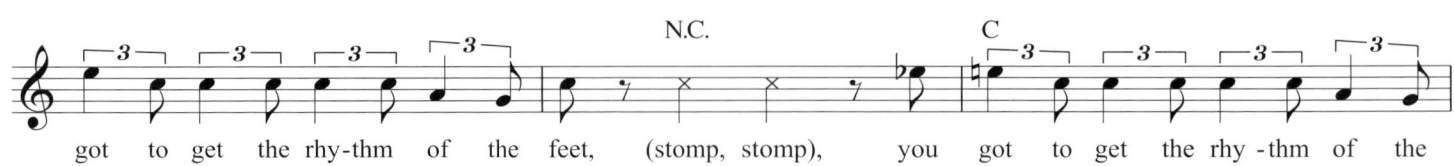

got to get the rhy-thm of the feet, (stomp, stomp), you got to get the rhy-thm of the

feet, (stomp, stomp)." Talked to the her-on, and the her-on said, "You

got to get the rhy-thm of the oys - ter, you got to get the rhy-thm of the

oys - ter." Put it all to-geth - er and, what - ta you got? "Ding,

dong, (clap, clap), (stomp, stomp), oys - ter." Turn it a-round back-ward and,

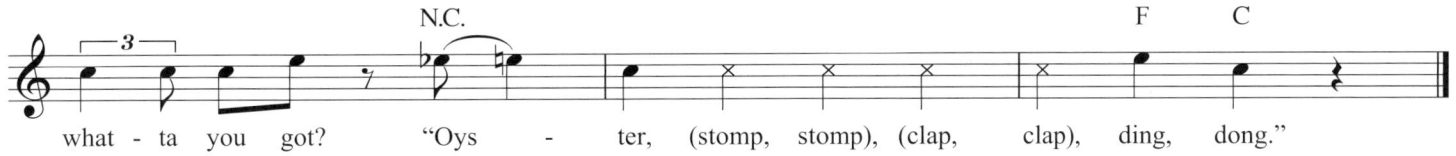

what - ta you got? "Oys - ter, (stomp, stomp), (clap, clap), ding, dong."

NOTE: This song is usually sung acapella. Simple musical accompaniment optional.
On "Ding, dong," tilt head left, then right. On "Oyster," make large circle with knees and hips.

The Land Mary-land

"Your dreams are like the mainsail set high upon the mast,

and you'll run before the free winds, as long as dreams can last.

My sails are blowed and torn, laid down wet.

They need all the mendin' that they can get.

There's no time to be attendin' 'cause the wind's alive today,

These sails are worn and weathered and I'm bound to go my way."

—"Blowed and Torn," song by Tom Wisner

SONGS

Dredgin' Is My Drudgery • The graceful wooden vessels of the Chesapeake are the last fleet of working boats under sail in America. From fall to spring, they harvest oysters from the Bay. It is dangerous, cold and exhausting work, but hard toil and a sense of pride in the work is a hallmark of the Chesapeake oystermen. Once there were between 600-800 working boats, but with the deterioration of the oyster population, now there are less than ten.

Hard Times (Board of a Drudgeboat) • Cap'm Alex Kellam taught Tom this song. "Cap'm" is a Chesapeake term.

Lay Me In The Forepeak • *"Cap'm Watt Herbert passed on this song to me that he learned in 1920 from Cap'm Charlie Foster of Colonial Beach, VA. In the hard times following the Civil War, men were enticed to go down into Tangier Sound and southern Chesapeake to work all winter. At the end of the season, Cap'm order a man to work atop the cabin, and once he was there, Cap'm would lay off the helm and the boat would go into a jibe. The boom would sweep across the deck at a very high velocity, and knock the sailor into the frigid waters. The Cap'm would just sail away, leaving that sailor out in the shoal waters to walk ashore. Folks would say, 'Well that fellow was paid off by the boom.'"*

Susquehanna Down • *"When my oldest son Mark was only 17, he worked aboard Cap'm Stan Daniels' oysterin' skipjack, The Howard. It was hard work in the frigid cold, and he was in awe of those great Island watermen. He wrote this song with verses about Cap'm Stan and his father Cap'm Art Daniels, and Cap'm Susanna Brinsfield of Solomons, one of the few female captains. Mark now follows the fish in Alaska."*

The Land Mary-land • *"A song inspired by the 139th Psalm about our coming to America. One of Maryland's first arriving ships, The Dove, is believed to have been named from this psalm. 'On the wings of the morning' is the symbol of The Dove."*

Dredgin' Is My Drudgery

Words and Music by
TOM WISNER

♩ = 80

Chorus

Dredg - in' is my drudg - er - y, ___ sail - in' is my pride; ___ I

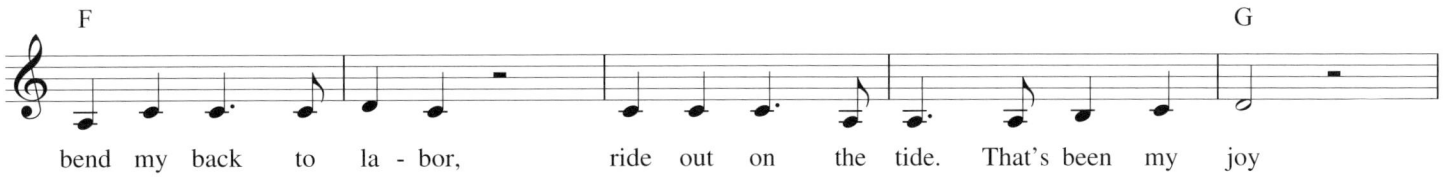

bend my back to la - bor, ride out on the tide. That's been my joy

Verse

since I'se a boy.   1. When the sum - mer ___ sun is rest - in', 'n' the
2. *See additional lyrics*

crabs are set - tl - in' down, ___ trees are turn - in' rust - ed, and the marsh is burnt to

brown. I long to feel the tim - bers ___ of a ves - sel ___ brought to life, ___

___ by rest - less winds and hard - y men ___ who join me in my plight.

Additional Lyrics

2. I plow the sea on Monday, push on Tuesday too.
Wednesday is a sailing day, and I start missing you.
On Thursday I get weary, as we lick across that rock;
start to pray for Friday when we put her to the dock.
Chorus

3. Come March I'm feeling weary and I long to go ashore;
my knees are growin' heels and toes, my back is bent and sore.
I've culled two-thousand bushels and I'm rusted to the bone,
wind and water whistles where my muscles used to roam.
Chorus

Hard Times (Board of a Drudge Boat)

Traditional

Verse

♩. = 60

(Jaw harp)* *Repeat 3 times*

* Playing an instrument as a rhythmic drone throughout this song is an option for accompaniment. The root note C is suggested.

1. The food that they give you, _____ it ain't much to
2. *See additional lyrics*

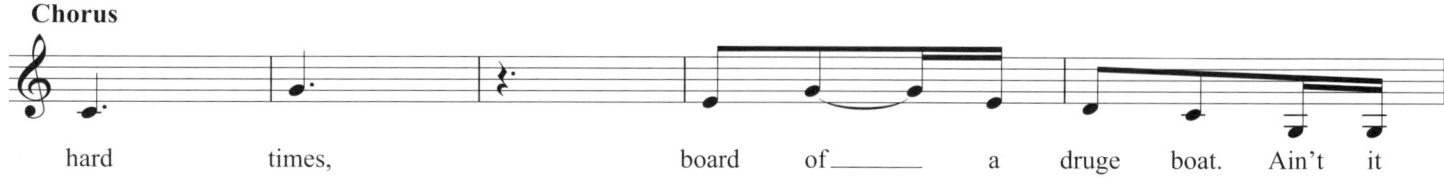

eat. Cook mix it up with his big dirt - y feet. Oh, it's

Chorus

hard times, board of _____ a druge boat. Ain't it

hard times to fol - low this wa - ter? _____

Additional Lyrics

2. I got one big longin', neither nary nor high,
I will follow this water and live 'til I die.

3. I drink me own fixin's, I fight fair and free.
If you don't like my apples, then don't shake my tree.

4. Pack up my songs; take my jaw bow,
and make me self welcome wherever I go.

5. Nobody to push me, no reason to bawl.
Best on this water, got no boss at all!

6. They fixes some meat, but it ain't much of that.
It's mostly some bone and a good side of fat.

7. They say that I'm ornery, bare as a bone.
Them what don't like me can leave me alone.

Lay Me In the Forepeak

Words and Music Adapted by
TOM WISNER with CAP'M WATT HERBERT

Chorus & Verses

$\downarrow = 80$

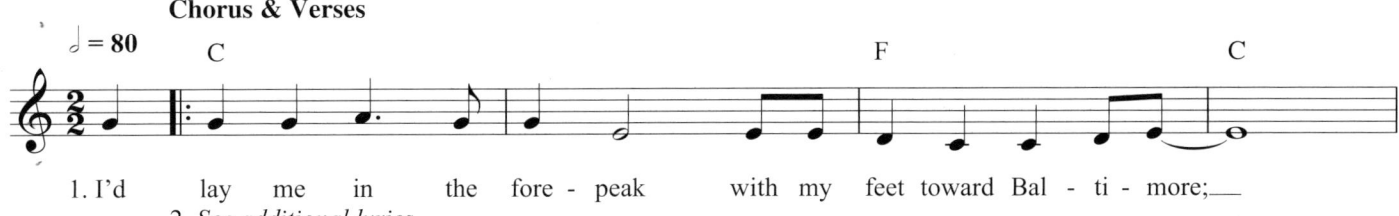

1. I'd lay me in the fore-peak with my feet toward Bal - ti - more;
2. *See additional lyrics*

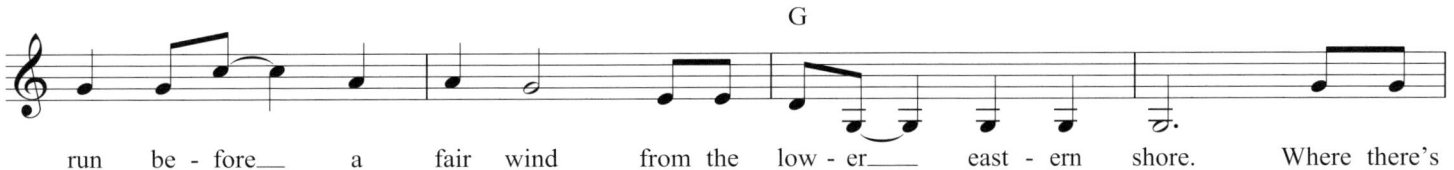

run be - fore___ a fair wind from the low - er___ east - ern shore. Where there's

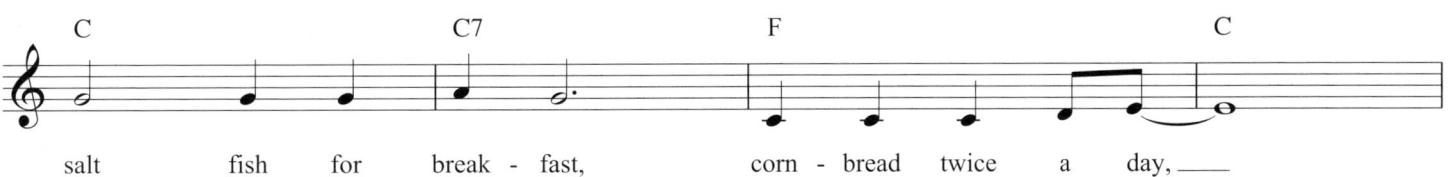

salt fish for break - fast, corn - bread twice a day, ___

you're a luck - y drudg - er if you nev - er___ get your pay.___ *See additional lyrics*

___ You're a luck - y drud - ger if you nev - er___ get your pay.___

Additional Lyrics

2. 'Cause when the captain pays you, it may be your doom.
   Ride to meet your maker out before a jib and boom,
   (and you will) swallow cold, grey water, wash up on the shore,
   give up all your longing for the port of Baltimore.
   Chorus

3. Keep your eye upon the helmsman when his vessel's running free.
   Leave here with the life you have, that's all the pay there'll be.
   When the season's over in 1885,
   kneel and count your blessings, be grateful you're alive.
   Chorus

Susquehanna Down

**Words and Music by
MARK WISNER**

Chorus

♩ = 64

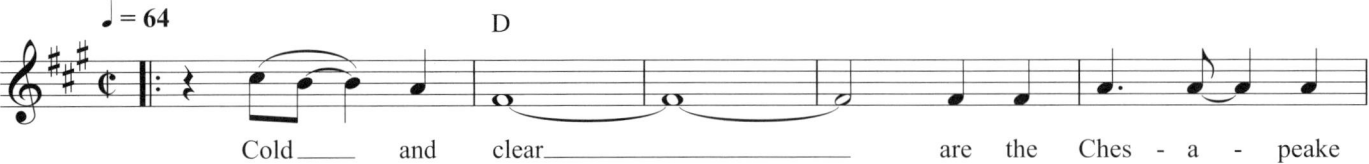

Cold___ and clear_____ are the Ches - a - peake

wa - ters,_____ free are__ the men,_____ who

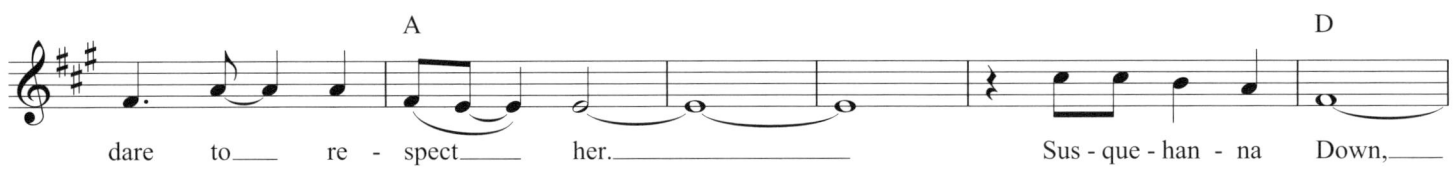

dare to__ re - spect__ her._____ Sus - que - han - na Down,___

_____ to o - cean wa - ters in Vir - gin - ia,_____ you'll car - ry

Fine

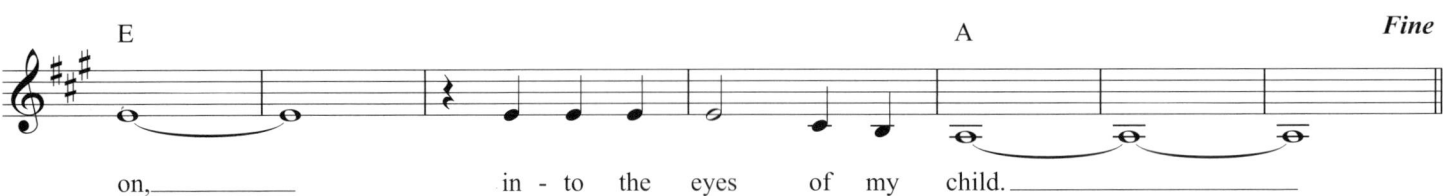

on,_____ in - to the eyes of my child._____

Verse

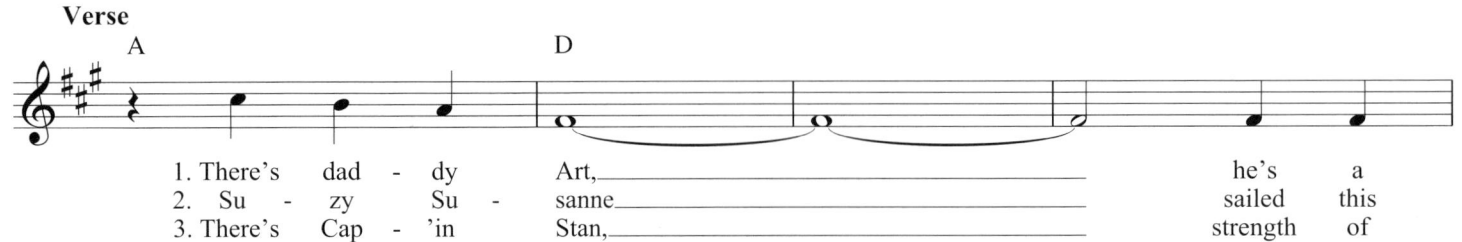

1. There's dad - dy Art,_____ he's a
2. Su - zy Su - sanne_____ sailed this
3. There's Cap - 'in Stan,_____ strength of

The Land Mary-land

Words and Music by
TOM WISNER

♩ = 138

Chorus

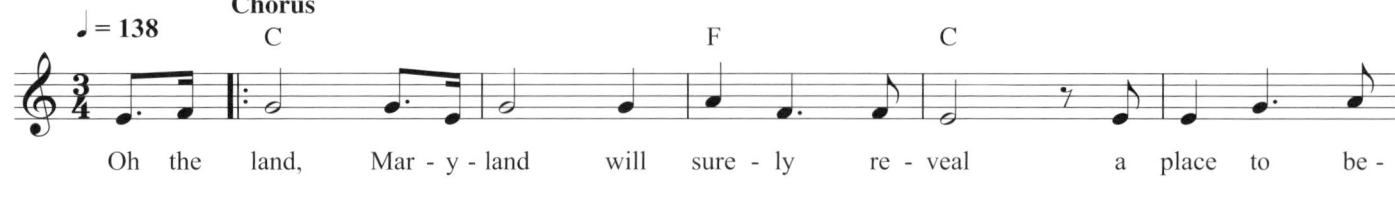

Oh the land, Mar - y - land will sure - ly re - veal a place to be -

lieve in the truth that we feel. On the wings of the morn - ing in the

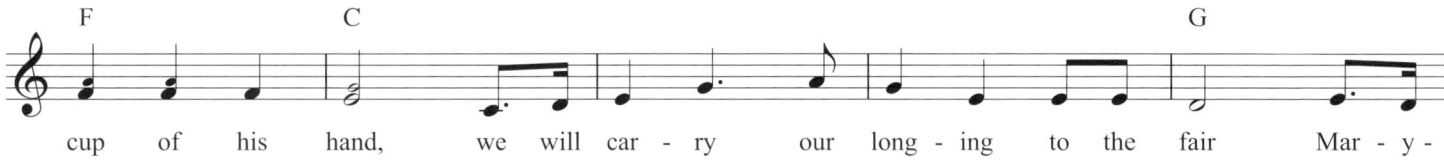

cup of his hand, we will car - ry our long - ing to the fair Mar - y -

Verse

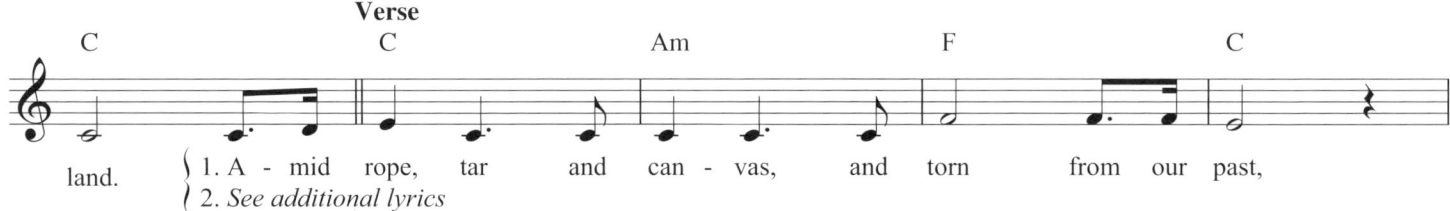

land. 1. A - mid rope, tar and can - vas, and torn from our past,
2. *See additional lyrics*

in a dun - geon of tim - ber we pray we may last. Through sick - ness and tur - moil in

search of our home, trust our con - vic - tion to the roll - ing white foam. For the

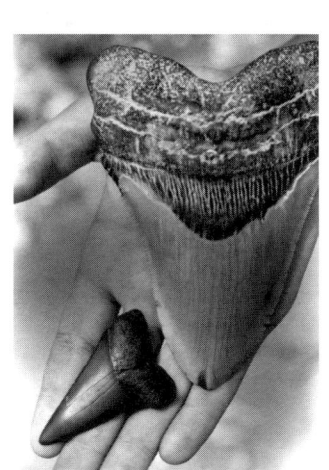

Additional Lyrics

2. She is rigged out and handsome, a maid of the sea,
   bound on a journey for humanity.
   She'll sail through the morning to the great ocean wide,
   bearing the longing that is carried inside.
   Chorus

3. Long before I was made in the depths of the earth,
   You knew of my longing and you fashioned my birth.
   With a passion to journey out over the sea
   in seach of the vision of the right to live free.
   Chorus

"We are bound in a web of deep and mysterious relations with the souls of other creatures. ...they are the wonderful elements of the creation that haunt, nourish and guide our lives... periwinkles, crabs, fish, goose, the terrapin, the great blue heron and relentless old watermen."

"See the great life in those river lines flowin' down out of the eyes of the likes of Cap'm Susanna Brinsfield."

"There is majesty and wonder in the great community of life that is called CHESAPEAKE. My sense of wonder has grown through deepening connection to the oral traditions, visions and mantras of the elemental people."

Tom sought out those who "followed on the water" and understood deeply the patterns and seasons of Chesapeake water ways. From people like Cap'ms Windbon Joy, Spearman Lancaster, Susanna Brinsfield, Art Daniels, Watt Herbert, Alex Kellam, and Martin O'Berry, Tom learned stories of wisdom, humor and knowledge that is now becoming extinct. He also found friendship.

"Cap'm Alex Kellam told me, 'Every time I get ready to sing one of the old songs or tell one of their stories, I feel all those who have come before me standing right behind me.'"

—Tom Wisner

Follow the Way

*"When we'd travel home from school
we'd linger by the streams and pools
to sing a rosy minnow melody.
Talk to crawdads, dance with frogs,
and walk across on wobbly logs
to celebrate the soul in every woodland thing!
One day round a shady bend
I became the water's friend
And we promised to carry to the end.
Oh carry me now!
Winding river water carry me!"*

—"Carry Me," song by Tom Wisner

"When I was a boy I played with my friends by a stream running through the outer borders of Washington, D.C. …it became my source of deeply felt values. The creatures of the stream were as much my friends as (were) my human friends. Such places we love as a child can fashion within us a sense of justice.

Imagination has a powerful role in our learning about our relationship with the natural world! Through wonder and imagination we choose, become, breathe and speak as that other person, creature or place."

SONGS

Tremchamblin • *"For my daughter Karen Leigh. The imagery of Tremchamblin is an attempt to create a mythology that may nourish the creative imagery of young and old alike. Children could enjoy doing drawings and stories about this magical horse and their imagined journeys on his back. You could also sing (or write new verses), 'You can ride out oe'r the great blue sea, become any creature that you want to be. Wade into a tidal pool, join the fishes on their way to school.'"*

The Knarly Monster • Imagination can transform fear into joyful discoveries.

Tumble In the Sun • *"There is pleasure and peace in appreciating the life around us."*

Come Full Circle • A song for the dance of life. Tom founded "Mother of the Waters Puppet Theatre," and he built "Chesepioc," a puppet with a magnificent and benevolent 8 ft. face and two separate 4 ft. hands. She could hug 20 children at one time. She was named after the "Chesepioc" native peoples, whose name meant "Mother of the Waters."

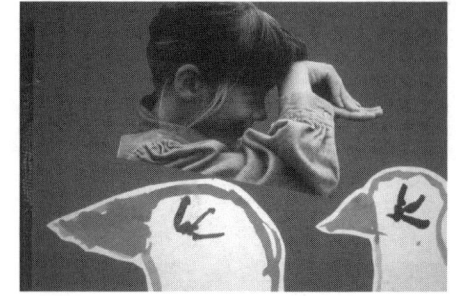

Follow The Way • A song about trusting wisdom of the heart and finding one's own way.

Tremchamblin

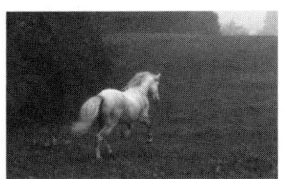

Words and Music by
TOM WISNER

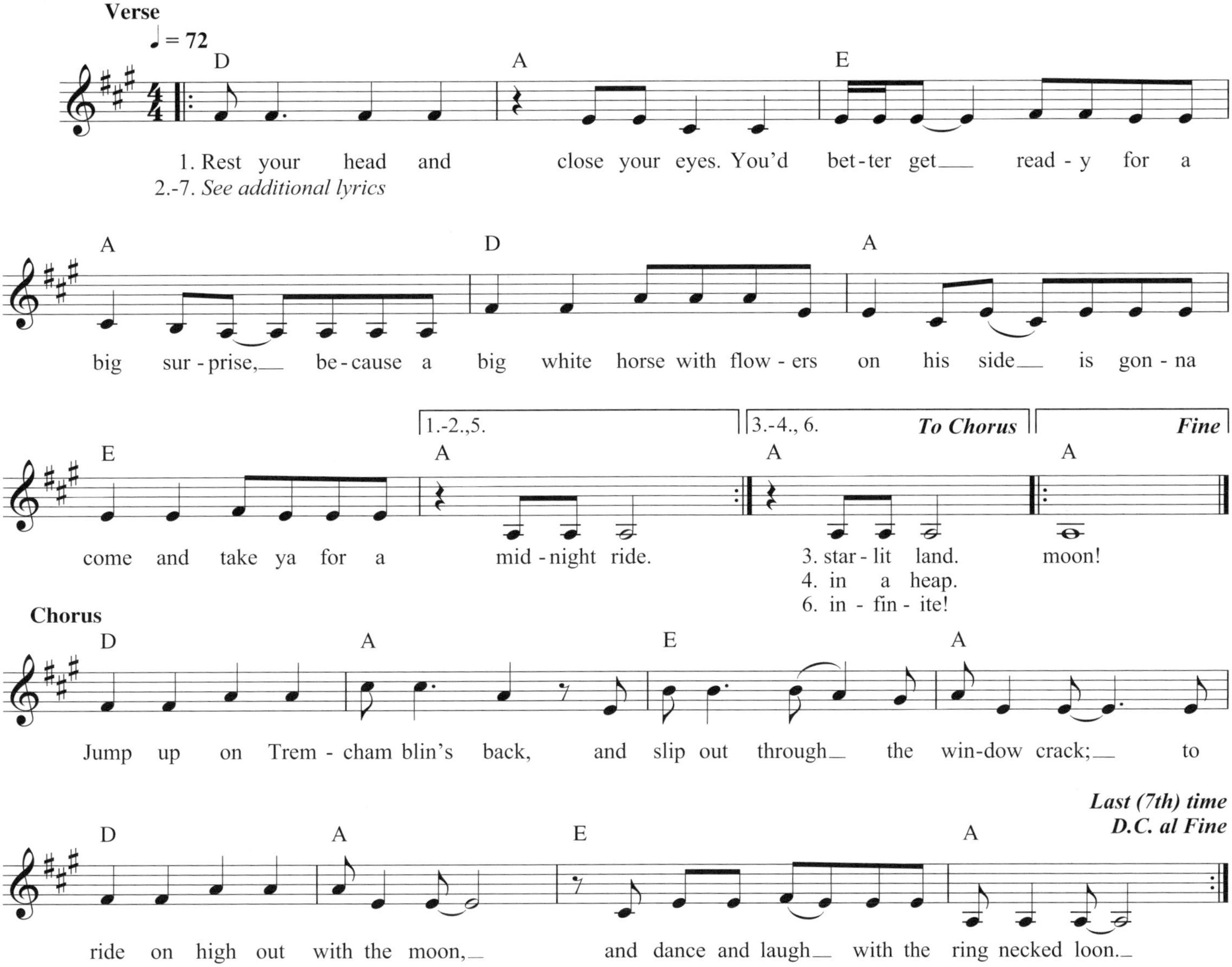

Verse
♩ = 72
D A E
1. Rest your head and close your eyes. You'd bet-ter get___ read - y for a
2.-7. *See additional lyrics*
A D A
big sur - prise,___ be-cause a big white horse with flow - ers on his side___ is gon - na
1.-2.,5.
3.-4., 6.
To Chorus
Fine
E A A A
come and take ya for a mid - night ride.
3. star - lit land.
4. in a heap.
6. in - fin - ite!
moon!
Chorus
D A E A
Jump up on Trem - cham blin's back, and slip out through___ the win-dow crack;___ to
Last (7th) time
D.C. al Fine
D A E A
ride on high out with the moon,___ and dance and laugh___ with the ring necked loon.___

Additional Lyrics

2. Tremchamblin is his stately name,
 imagination is his game.
 For when you're up upon his back
 there's hardly anything you lack.

3. You can talk to flowers and to trees,
 sing off key with the buzzin' bees.
 Nature talk at your command
 as you prance across the starlit land.
 Chorus

4. Each night before you go to sleep,
 he'll appear and bound and leap.
 And the old folks, they'll drift off to sleep,
 while the children dance the covers up in a heap.
 Chorus

5. When finished with your nightly ride,
 you'll melt through walls and be inside.
 He'll nip your hair and pinch your ear so
 you won't remember that he was here.

6. Most folks would laugh with a knowing look
 if you told them of the ride you took.
 But if you believe, then the fire is lit.
 You see…imagination makes you infinite.
 Chorus

7. Youth is made for wonderin',
 and I grow old too soon.
 Hey, I wish I could slip back and
 RIDE… ride with the man in the moon.

The Knarly Monster

Words and Music by
TOM WISNER

1. Do you be-lieve in bats and cav-ey plac-es; spook-ey
2., 3. *See additional lyrics*

space-es, where the kook-y, knar-ly night-time crea-tures

creep? Can you feel the chill of dark-ness all a-round— you?

It sur-rounds you; oh, you dare not go to sleep.

For the crea-tures of the night time are out there cir-cling

'round. One is bound to eat you while the oth-ers hold you

down. Well, I will not fear the dark-ness or the crea-tures of the

Chorus 2: *See additional lyrics*

night, be - cause in my be - liev - ing I will turn them towards the

light. So go home, you knar - ly mon - ster, take your drip - py teeth and

claws, and put them in the pock - et of your bag - gy o - ver -

alls. If you don't go, I will change you to a wig - gly lit - tle worm, and

put you in the gar - den where the earth is dark and firm. 2. Can you
3. Well, I

Additional Lyrics

2. Can you make your home in earthy, cavey places; Spooky spaces,
and cuddle with the pearly clumps of clay?
Can you crawl down in the earth and get it moving,
growing, grooving, making ready for the happy rains of May?
Leafy fingers peeking up and reaching for the sun,
while roots are getting water from where the work was done.

Chorus 2

Well, I will not fear the darkness or the creatures of the night,
because in my believing I will turn them towards the light.
And the garden is a greeny place where candy colors bloom,
while the Knarly monster steals from the darkness of my room,
oh, the Knarly monster steals from the darkness of my room.

Tumble in the Sun

Words and Music by
TERESA WHITAKER
and TOM WISNER

Chorus

♩ = 120

Tum-ble in the sun, warm earth roll-in' by,

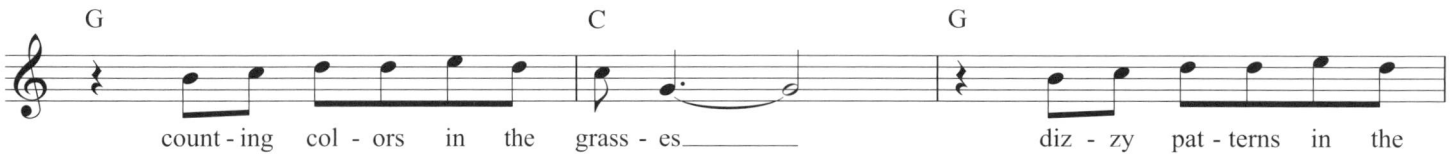

count-ing col-ors in the grass-es dizzy pat-terns in the

Fine   **Verse**

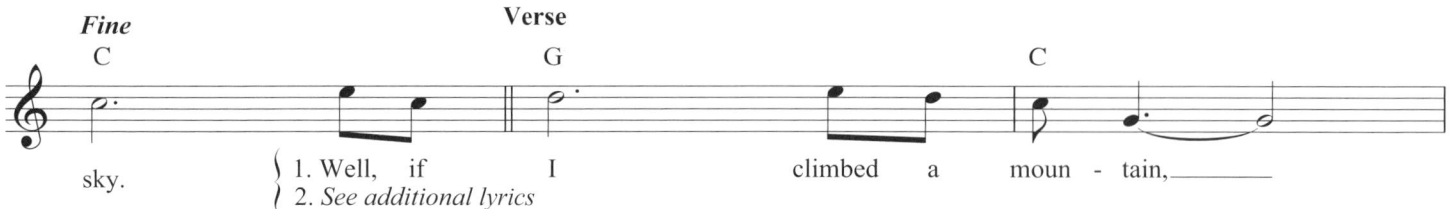

sky.

1. Well, if I climbed a moun-tain,
2. *See additional lyrics*

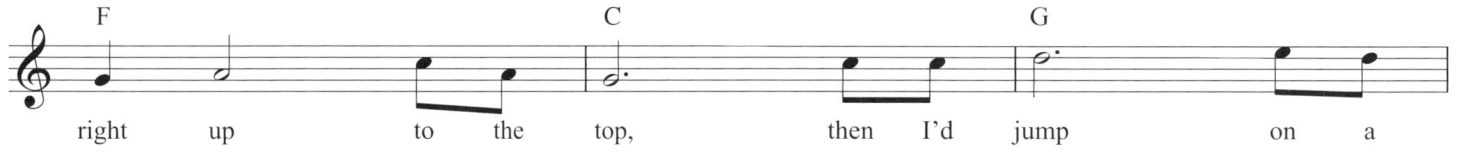

right up to the top, then I'd jump on a

cloud and I'd ride un-til I stopped.

Additional Lyrics

2. Oh, a tree drinks the water, throws its hands up to the sky;
secret places in its branches where the young birds learn to fly.
Chorus

Bernie's Measure

All the politicians gathered: they'd come from miles around
to talk about the river that flows by Solomon's town.
Seems they had a problem, things were looking bad.
They'd looked at all the resources, used everything they had.

The scientists had told them everything they knew.
Still, the folks were puzzled and they didn't know what to do.
It came 'round to Bernie Fowler and he stood among the best.
He said, "Folks, if you'll bear with me I think I've got a test,

I think I have a measure that can't be beat:
you just wade out in the river and look down at your feet.
If you can't see your cloppers, there'll be trouble in this town.
We ought a sue those upper counties for the junk they're sending down."

It's Bernie's measure and it ain't hard to do.
It's a pleasure, and it will soothe you too.
You just wade out in the river—give it all you got,
right up to your chest and then you pick your spot.
Next you take your peepers and cast them slowly down.
On the day we see our feet again there'll be celebration in this town.

We should do this yearly on Bernie Fowler Day:
dress up fit to kill and wade out all the way.
And somewhere in the future that day is coming sure,
we'll look and see our feet again; could we ask for more?
I ask you what's the profit if we gain these worldly things
and foul the air and water and all the life they bring.

Photo by Hillary Harp

— Tom Wisner, written for the first "Patuxent Wade In." (From Sara Leeland's book *Gather 'Round Chesapeake*, credit page 56). The "Wade In" has happened every June since 1988. It is a communal ritual begun by former Maryland State Senator Bernie Fowler.

Come Full Circle

Words and Music by
TOM WISNER

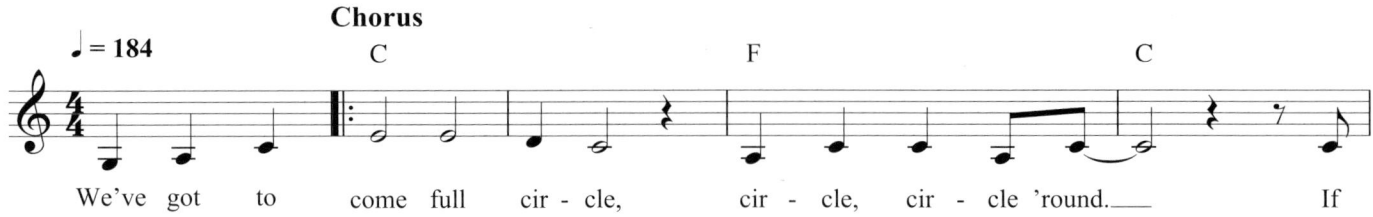

Chorus

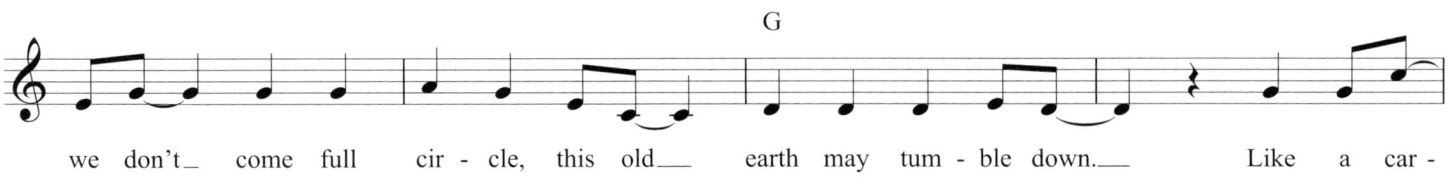

We've got to come full cir - cle, cir - cle, cir - cle 'round.___ If

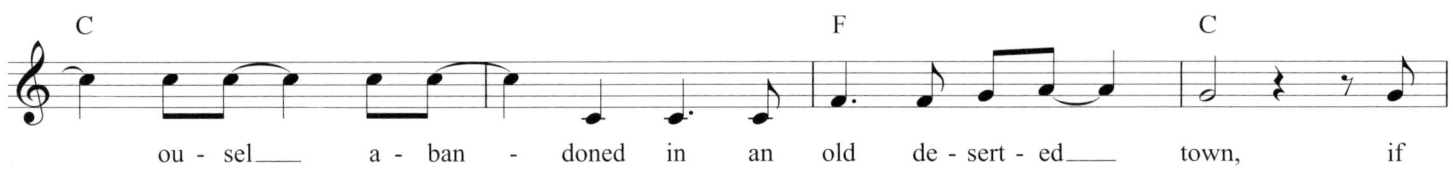

we don't_ come full cir - cle, this old___ earth may tum - ble down.___ Like a car -

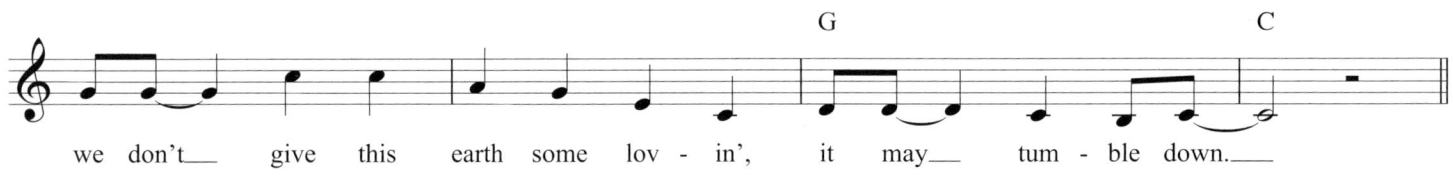

ou - sel___ a - ban - doned in an old de - sert - ed___ town, if

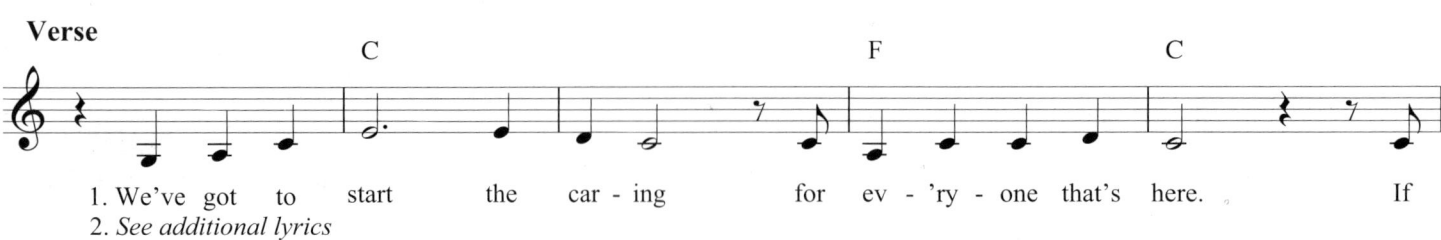

we don't___ give this earth some lov - in', it may___ tum - ble down.___

Verse

1. We've got to start the car - ing for ev - 'ry - one that's here.   If
2. *See additional lyrics*

we don't love_ one an - oth - er, we may_ dis - ap - pear.___ Ev - 'ry sin - gle

per - son   has   their   dig - ni - ty,_____   and   the   right__   to

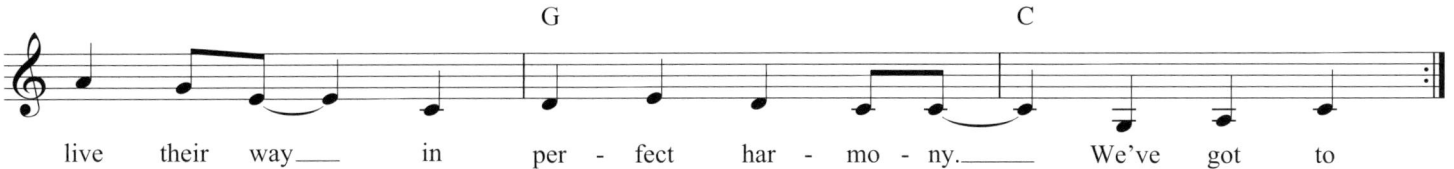

live   their   way____   in   per - fect   har - mo - ny._____   We've   got   to

Additional Lyrics

2. We've got to start the sharing of our quality;
   join in the believing that the sharing sets us free.
   Every truth that's realized and uttered by a soul
   has a value to be shared and the sharing makes us whole.
   Chorus

3. We've got to start the caring for all the life that's here;
   if we don't love the creatures they may disappear.
   Every single creature has its dignity
   and the right to live it out in perfect harmony.
   Chorus

"Our remarkable, diverse and beautiful planet needs diversity of mind and heart."

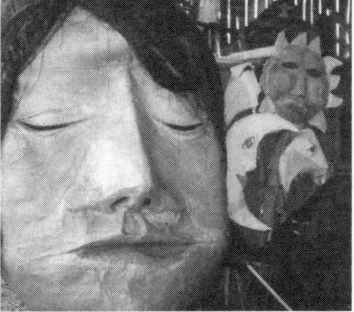

Photo by Margo Coffin Groff

"Become a participant in the mystery of creation, in the health of the Bay. Give yourself to the circle as best you can."

—Tom Wisner

Follow the Way

Words and Music by
TOM WISNER

Chorus

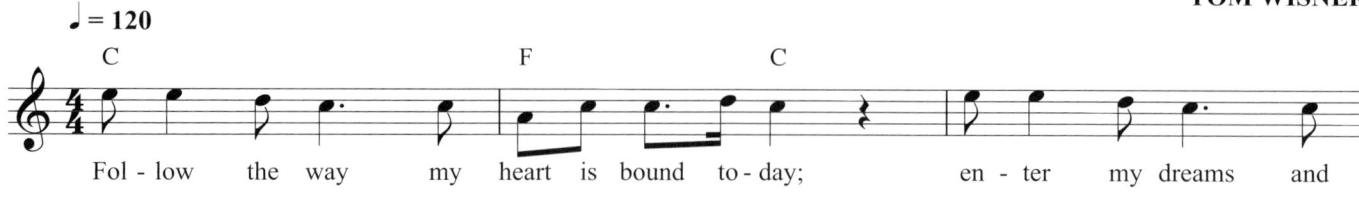

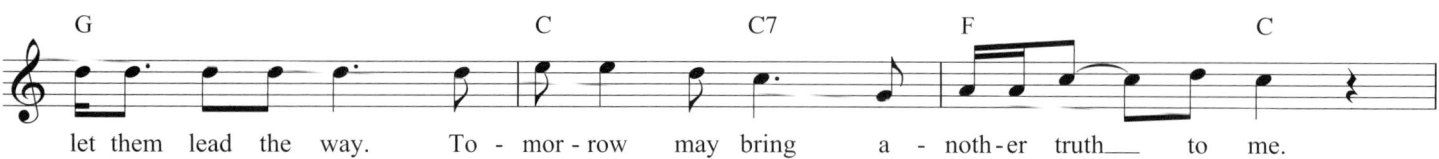

Fol - low the way my heart is bound to-day; en - ter my dreams and

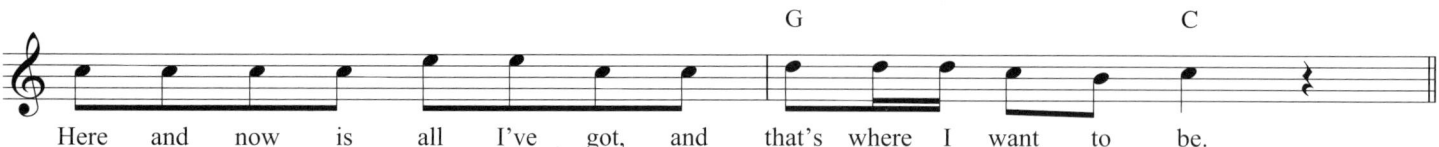

let them lead the way. To - mor - row may bring a - noth-er truth to me.

Here and now is all I've got, and that's where I want to be.

Verse

1. If I were a cold lit - tle bird, hud - dlin' on a wire, I'd reach up and touch the sun and

2., 3. *See additional lyrics*

catch my - self some fire. Be I bird up - on a wire long - in' for the sun;

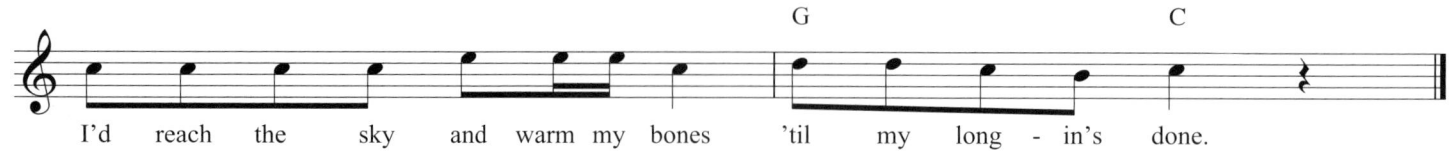

I'd reach the sky and warm my bones 'til my long - in's done.

Additional Lyrics

2. If I was a potato snugglin' in the ground
   I would want to be the best potato 'round.
   Be I big or be I round potato in the ground,
   grow I good, I'm bound to be the best potato round.
   Chorus

3. I am where I am right now no matter where I be.
   If I could be someone else, I would just be me.
   Be I big or be I small, be I laugh or cry,
   I will be just what I am and live until I die.
   Chorus

Chesapeake Born

"Hope lies in bringing forth the truth about the Chesapeake Bay and placing our awareness right next to the issues.

We'll save the river when every child in the watershed discovers what he or she loves about the river, and finds a way to share that love."

—Tom Wisner

SONGS

Esta Tierra de las Aguas • This song was translated into Spanish by Julian Jasso. One group of early native people in the Bay was called "Chesepioc" (K'che-sepiak). Their name was thought to have come from the great bay to the north of them, and meant, "The Mother of Waters." The early Spanish explorers called the Bay, "La Bajia de la Santa Maria." Combining these ideas, this song imagines the Patuxent River speaking in Spanish, to people then and now. As Tom said, "I believe the river has spoken to all people, reminding us that the waters are a great source of life to be cared for, in any time and place."

All Souls Sing • Maryland's diamondback terrapins are estuarine turtles (living in brackish waters), and they have long been part of Maryland's history. With their ancient eyes and beautiful patterned shells, they have survived for centuries. But now, due to a combination of environmental stresses and aspects of their own life cycles, they are in danger. (See www.arlingtonecho.org for info on their amazing Chesapeake Connections program.)

Wild River • "A river is a symbol of all living things. A river, like a person deserves our care. It is powerful to think of our relationship to a particular river as we would think of our relationship to our friends, or parents or teachers. It's all a matter of how we look at it. If we imagine the river as having a voice, what could it teach us? If we take from the river, what will we give back?"

Cap'm Gone • "This song pays tribute to the wisdom, resilience and humor of the elemental people who are the unique human character of Bay life and Chesapeake water ways. They are the voices of these waters!"

Freedom is a River (Chorus) • This is part of a much longer song of the same name. Tom often showed children a map of the Chesapeake watershed and all its rivers. Then he would use whole body gestures to show the shape of each river flowing to the Bay. Moving fluidly from one river gesture to the next, he called this a "Tai Chi of the rivers." The children all joined in chanting the names and moving the rivers' shapes.

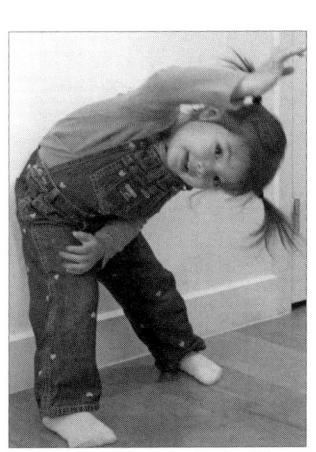

Chesapeake Born • "Chesapeake Born was written with the entire watershed in mind. It is about the shed of 40 river 'children' that drain into the 'mother' Chesapeake."

Photo by Karina Glaser

Esta Tierra de las Aguas
(Land of the Waters)

Words and Music by
Tom Wisner

Chorus

♩ = 120

Es - ta ti - er - ra de las a - guas de la mad - re, de la mad - re de di -

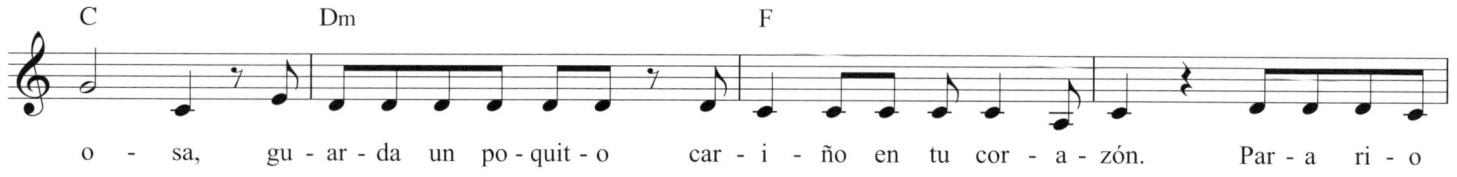

o - sa, gu - ar - da un po - quit - o car - i - ño en tu cor - a - zón. Par - a ri - o

mad - re___ y po - quit - o de ver - de par - a di - os,___ par - a di - os,

Last time to Coda ⊕ | **1. Verse**

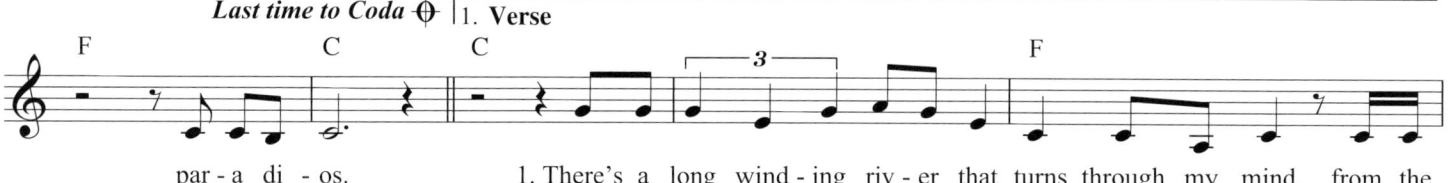

par - a di - os. 1. There's a long wind - ing riv - er that turns through my mind, from the

stor - ies she told by the light in my eye___ 'bout the act of cre - a - tion, the

birth of the sea in my soul. It's a stor - y comes down from green

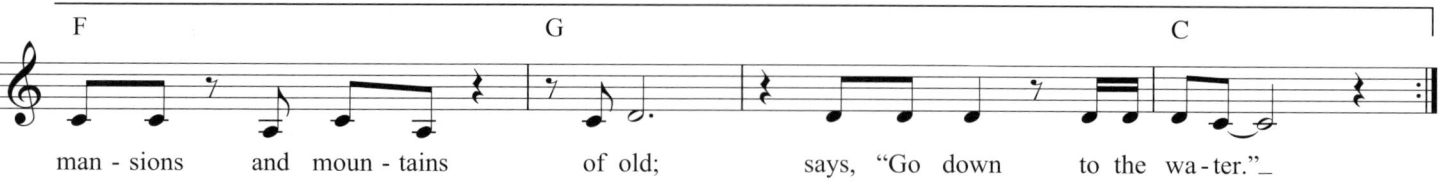

man - sions and moun - tains of old; says, "Go down to the wa - ter."___

All Souls Sing

Words and Music by
TOM WISNER

Verse

♩ = 84

1. Tur - tle called Sus - que - han - na, gon - na tra - vel far.
2. *See additional lyrics*

Born out of the Shen - an - do - ah, reach - in' for a star, far

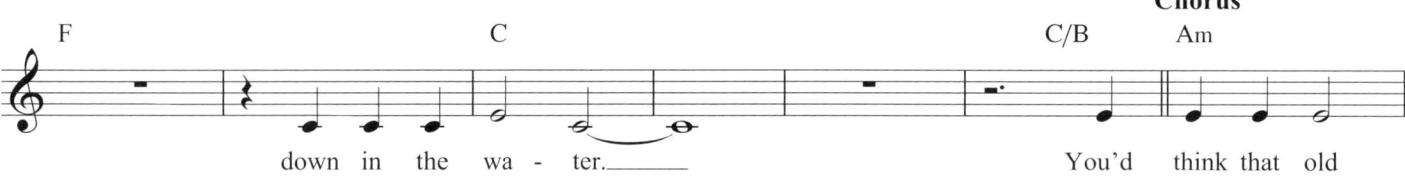

down in the wa - ter. You'd think that old

Chorus

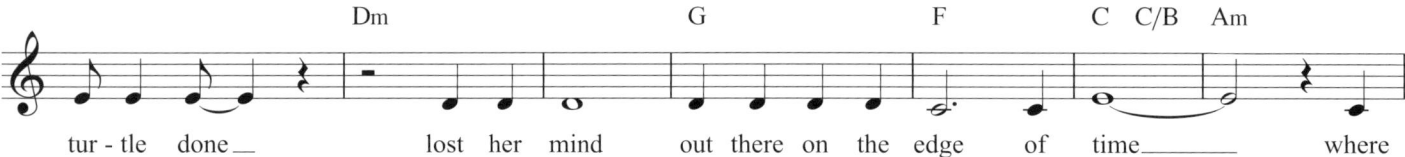

tur - tle done lost her mind out there on the edge of time where

all souls sing the songs; where all souls sing!

Additional Lyrics

2. Fire down in the ocean
   deep within the sea.
   Turtle gonna go and make it so,
   it's risin' up in me
   from far down in the water.
   Chorus

3. "Farewell" said Shad to Turtle.
   "Old Susquehanna down;
   gone out to the deep blue,
   to swim this world around
   from far down in the water."
   Chorus

4. From the darkness in the land
   sing where waters rise.
   Sing of Susquehanna,
   Susquehanna wise,
   from far down in the water.
   Chorus

Wild River

Words and Music by
TOM WISNER

1. Hey, there wild riv-er,___ teach me to flow.___
2. You're re-born each mo-ment,___ old as the land.___

Tell me your po-ems,___ and all the songs that you know.
No long-er flow-in',___ when you're cupped in my hand.

Touch me and wash me, and let me lie down,___
Join with my bod-y as I drink life's fill,___

by the peace of your wa-ters,___ at night on the ground.
and blend with these wa-ters,___ and flow as you will.

Chorus

Deep flow-in' riv - er, where are you bound?___ Tell me your

sto - ry_____ and teach me your sound.___ Hey, there wild riv-er,___

won't you teach me to flow?_____ Hey, won't you stop a laz-y

mo - ment while you're roll-in' a - long,_ and sing me your song?___

Cap'm Gone

**Words and Music by
TOM WISNER**

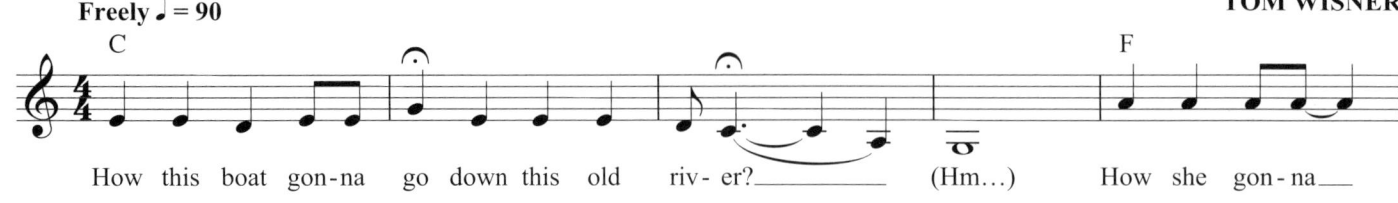

How this boat gon-na go down this old riv-er?_____ (Hm…) How she gon-na_____

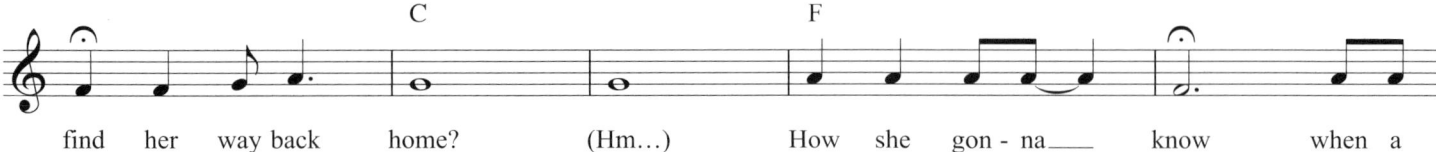

find her way back home? (Hm…) How she gon-na_____ know when a

cold wind gon-na blow? Cap-'m gone, that old Cap-'m, Cap-'m gone._____

1. How this boat gon-na go down this old riv-er?_____ How she gon-na
2., 3. *See additional lyrics*

find her way back home? (Hm…) How she gon-na know_____ when the

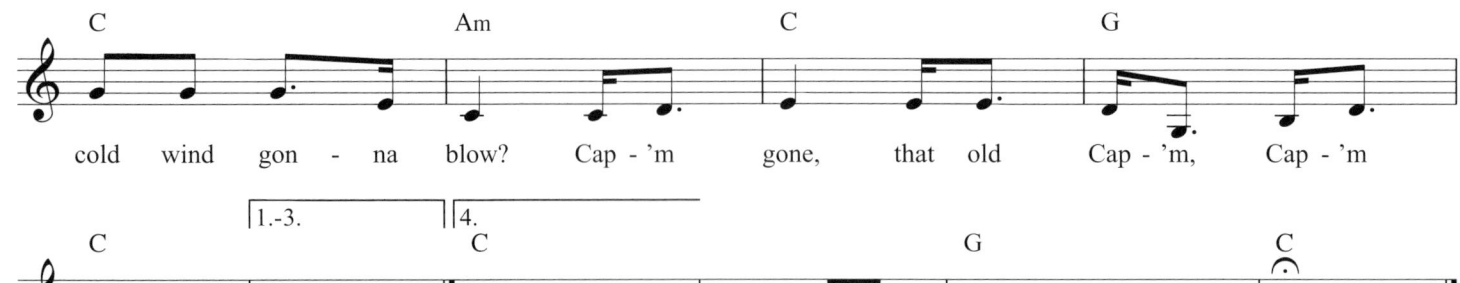

cold wind gon-na blow? Cap-'m gone, that old Cap-'m, Cap-'m

gone._____ _____ Cap-'m gone, that old Cap-'m, Cap-'m gone.

Additional Lyrics

2. What we gonna say to this old river?
   How we gonna tell her he has gone?
   How we gonna say, "That old Cap'm gone away?"
   Cap'm gone, that old Cap'm, Cap'm gone.

3. What we gonna do for this old river?
   How she gonna live without her friend?
   How she gonna find, lastin' peace of mind?
   Cap'm gone, that old Cap'm, Cap'm gone.

Freedom Is a River
(Chorus)

Words and Music by Tom Wisner

*"In our song there is a power, giving life to every word,
and high above the Chesapeake, the wind is often heard…singing:"*

Sus - que - han - na, Wi - co - mi - co South Se - vern, Nan - ti - coke

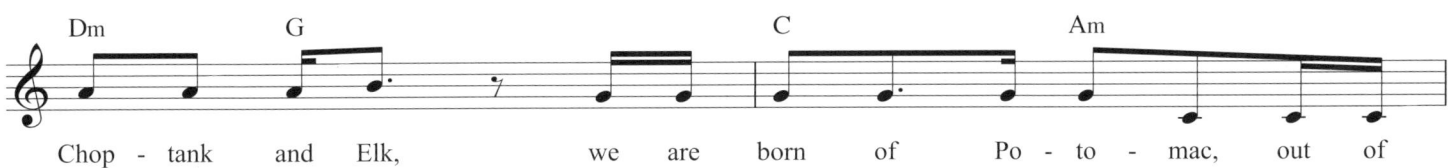

Chop - tank and Elk, we are born of Po - to - mac, out of

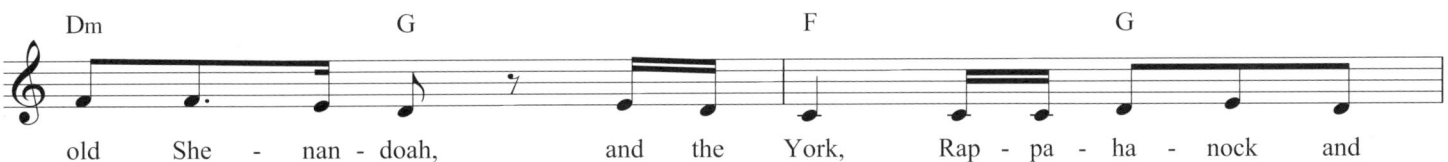

old She - nan - doah, and the York, Rap - pa - ha - nock and

James. the York, Rap - pa - han - ock and James.

"It is time we were giving the freedom of living to the rivers."

Chesapeake Born

Words and Music by
TOM WISNER

Chorus*

Swing ♩ = 110

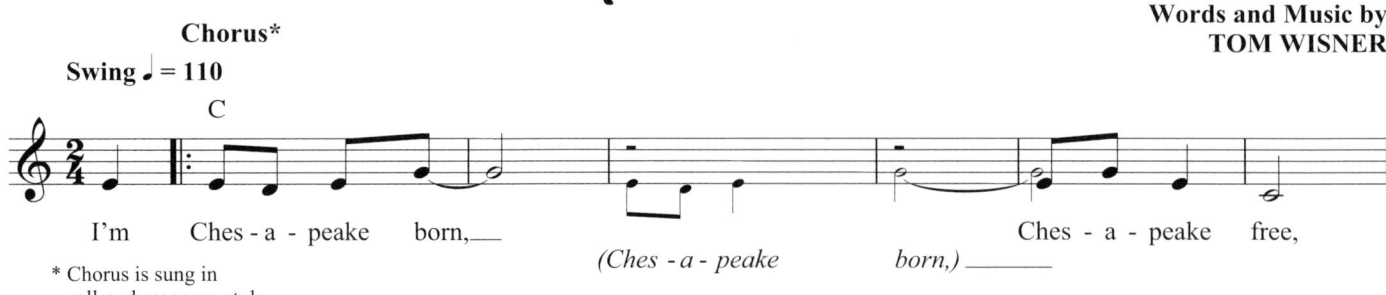

I'm Ches-a-peake born,___ (Ches-a-peake born,) Ches-a-peake free,

* Chorus is sung in call-and-response style.

(Ches-a-peake free,) I'm Ches-a-peake bound,___ (Ches-a-peake bound,) ___

flow-in' with ease. (Flow-in' with ease.) ___ I'm Ches-a-peake born. ___

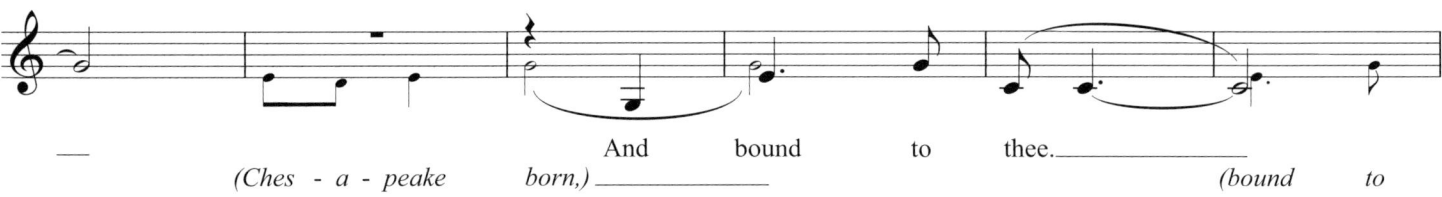

___ (Ches-a-peake born,) ___ And bound to thee. ___ (bound to

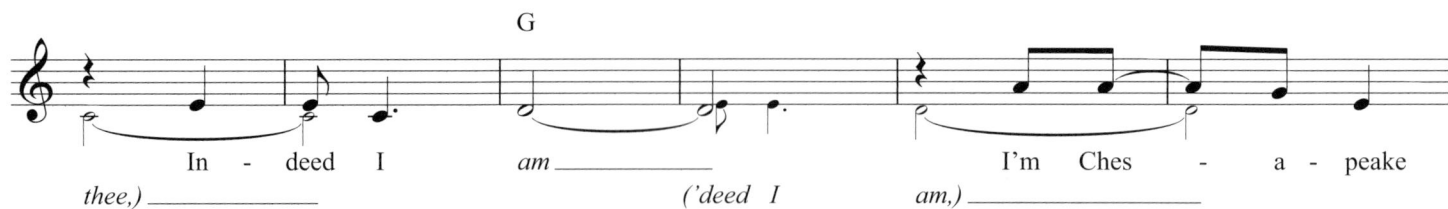

thee,) ___ In-deed I am ___ ('deed I am,) ___ I'm Ches-a-peake

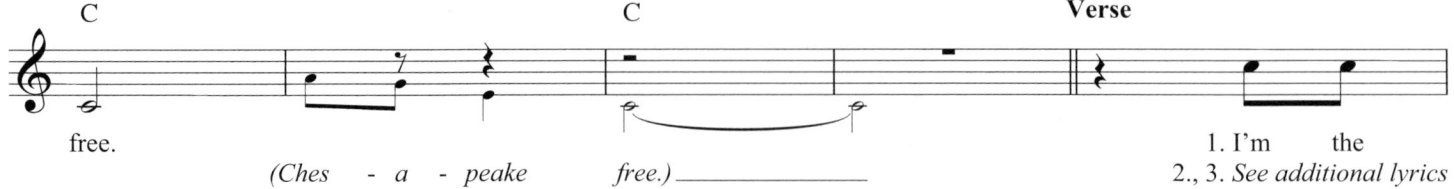

free. (Ches-a-peake free.) ___ 1. I'm the
2., 3. *See additional lyrics*

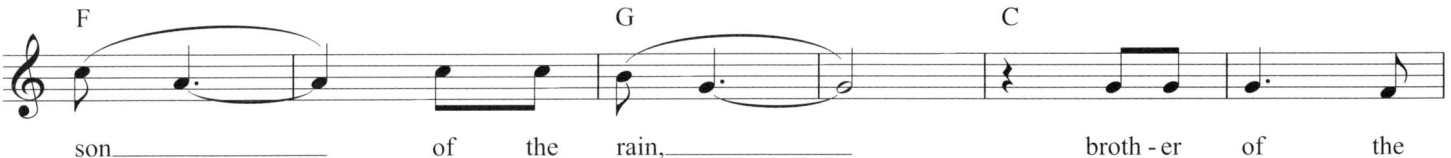

son_____ of the rain,_____ broth-er of the

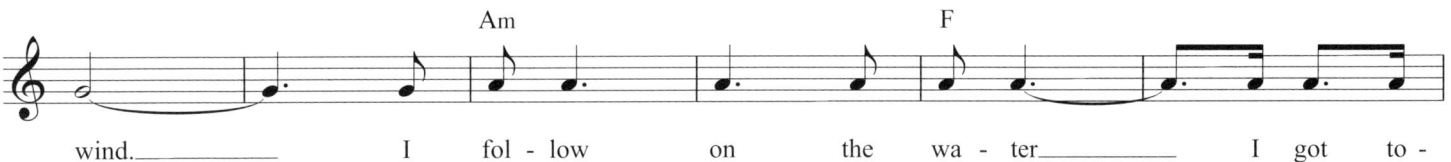

wind._____ I fol-low on the wa-ter_____ I got to-

bac-co__ on__ my chin, and I've seen__ for-ty years of

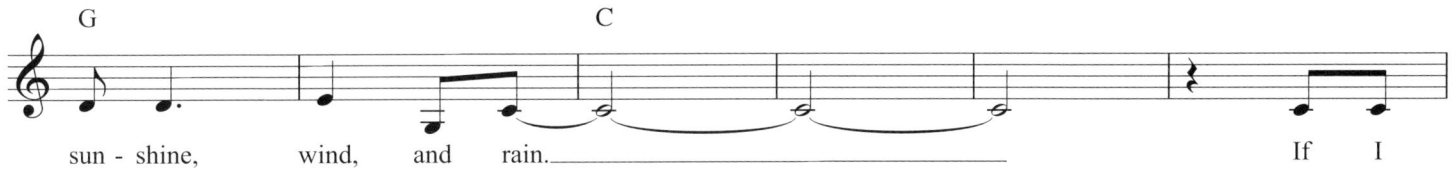

sun-shine, wind, and rain._____ If I

had the chance__ I'd do it_____ all a-gain._____ 'Cause I'm

Additional Lyrics

2. She's the Mother of the waters, and the people of this land;
   forty river children reach to take her by the hand,
   and flow through Maryland and Virginia to the sea.
   She's Atlantic born, Atlantic bound and free.
   Chorus

3. I hear your song so clearly and I know that down inside,
   the mother of these waters is a-flowing deep and wide.
   Sons and daughters of the water's life within,
   gentle voices blending with the wind.
   Chorus

What Are Songs For?

"You better watch the songs you sing...they will make you who you are!"

—Tom Wisner

"My songs are the result of a lifetime of thinking and teaching about a relationship to this land and its waters. I have a deep, steady and ongoing commitment to writing songs to celebrate the life of the Bay and her rivers.

Making songs is a way of seeking truth. In seeking my own truth, I have created symbols that represent life...not necessarily the way it is...but certainly the way I would like it to be. The ideal songs would sing of a balance between our life and the life of the Bay so that one would not bring destruction to the other. Such a song would have to be ever changing.

How are the beliefs and values about our relationship with the great community of life expressed in the lyrics of our songs? If you really want to know what a culture values and believes in, then go into schools and listen to what children are singing. Songs help us to form and sustain our values. They are a fine measure of who we are and where we are going.

There is a great sense of community created from singing together. It strengthens our hopes. What if all we had to do would be to cherish the planet and creation?

We are one with the earth. We are nourished in body and soul...made and re-made daily by a complex of miracles played out between ourselves and the soil, water, and air of the planet.

Ecology is not a subject. It is a new vision of reality! The way WE choose to shape our landscape will both reflect its shape, and shape the nature of ourselves. We live in a time when we are called to begin to create ways of thinking that are more in tune with our sense of unity within a greater story or song." —Tom Wisner

"You shine out like a beacon,

from the truth you're bound to live

and the beauty of all you've tried to give.

Songs of vision, songs of peace

Who will listen, who will speak?

Who will stand and sing?"

—"Stand and Sing," song for Tom Wisner,
by Teresa Whitaker and Frank Schwartz

Tom Wisner Biography

Tom Wisner (1930–2010)

Tom Wisner was a songwriter, musician, artist, photographer, poet, storyteller, puppeteer, environmental interpreter, and collector of oral history. Blending all of these gifts, he was also an exceptional environmental educator, synthesizing science and the arts in innovative ways.

He was born and grew up in the Anacostia section of Washington, D.C. There he rode steamboats to Mt. Vernon and Colonial Beach and sometimes camped with his father on the Virginia side of the Potomac River. Summers, he often visited with his mother's relatives on the Upper James River in Virginia. All of these experiences cultivated for him, a deep bond with waters.

He was part of the U.S. Air Force during the Korean War. Afterwards he earned a B.A. in science and did graduate work at Cornell University in biology and ecology. He was a National Park Service Naturalist at Sequoia National Park in the 1960's. He became Maryland's first environmental educator under the direction of Dr. L. Eugene Cronin, at the Chesapeake Biological Lab in Solomons, Maryland.

Ahead of his time, he discovered the power of the arts for conveying the complexities of science, and inspiring awareness and concern for the Bay. In 1978 Tom left the Lab and created a traveling "Chesapeake Classroom" which he continued for over thirty years. Using the arts, and modeling empathy and imagination, he enabled children to connect deeply to the Chesapeake Bay.

He won many awards including the "Maryland Governor's Citation" (by Gov. Harry Hughes), the "National Commission on the Out-of Doors Award" for national impact of regional education work, "Excellence in Teaching Award" from the University of Maryland, and "Outstanding Marine Educator of the Year Award" (Middle Atlantic Marine Education Assoc.), to name a few. For his music he was awarded a "Parents' Choice Award" and the World Folk Music Association's "John Denver Award." Tom's music, including his song, "Chesapeake Born" was featured in the National Geographic Special: "Chesapeake Borne" and in the Chesapeake Bay Foundation's film, "Living on the Edge." His earlier recordings are part of the Smithsonian Archive. In 1999 he co-founded with Sara Leeland, "CHESTORY": the Center for the Story of the Chesapeake. Its purpose is to bring the artist in everyone to express their role in the ongoing story of Chesapeake life and culture, and to bring communities into deeper relationship with Chesapeake river lands.

He spent a great part of his life devoted to raising awareness of the importance and uniqueness of the Chesapeake Bay and its more than forty tributary rivers and streams. For Tom, water was source, inspiration and teacher. To him, learning deeply about one's own "place" was the path to understanding the "whole." Focusing on the "watershed" meant honoring the importance of all species living there, and including all "voices," especially those of the waters themselves. For him "holistic education" meant understanding that all things connect, and that honoring these "connections," is essential for preserving the planet and the human spirit.

Contributor Biographies

ABOUT THE EDITORS

Jim Fox of Lion and Fox Recording Studios, Washington DC, is a master sound engineer. He worked with Tom on many of his albums and projects. He mastered the CD that accompanies this songbook and has been an invaluable co-creator of this project from the beginning. *(fox@lionfox.com)*

Kathleen W. Glaser was Principal of Hollywood Elementary School, where she worked with Tom Wisner for many years to bring meaningful and exciting environmental education and learning into children's lives. She is a recipient of the Washington Post Distinguished Leadership Award, and is a co-founder of the Chesapeake Public Charter School in Southern Maryland. She now serves as a Center for Courage and Renewal facilitator. She remains dedicated to children, schools and the environment. *(kwglaser@yahoo.com)*

Michael S. Glaser is a Professor Emeritus at St. Mary's College of Maryland where he often worked with Tom, and helped present Tom's work to a variety of audiences. Glaser served as a Maryland State Arts Council poet-in-the-schools for over 20 years, and serves on the Board of Directors of the Maryland Humanities Council, as well as the Maryland State Department of Education's Arts Advisory Committee. He served as Poet Laureate of Maryland from August 2004 through August 2009. *(msglaser@smcm.edu)*

Frank Schwartz a native of Baltimore, is a musician and singer songwriter who plays guitar, bass, old-time banjo and the mandolin. He is also fluent in sign language. On his own and also with his wife Teresa, he has recorded albums of original songs, most recently, "Finding Home." They are also co-creators of "Finding Home Publishing Company." He has long supported Tom's music, and his guitar, banjo and bass, (as well as his soulful voice) are part of many of Tom's recordings. *(www.frankschwartz.com* and *ftzj@cox.net)*

Teresa Whitaker was born in Kentucky. She is a singer, songwriter, and storyteller who offers school residencies and teacher workshops. She performs in schools, libraries, universities, hospitals, and at festivals and conferences. She also does extensive work with parents and lullabies. She collaborated and performed with Tom Wisner for many years, and her songs and voice can be heard on all of Tom's albums. She and her husband Frank travel and perform together. In addition to their own songs, they are carrying forward the legacy of Tom's music and environmental work and are available for workshops. They have two children. *(www.teresawhitaker.com* and *ftzj@cox.net)*

Mark Wisner was born on the banks of the Susquehanna River. His childhood years were spent chasing blue crab and striped bass from a 12 ft. skiff on Coles Creek. Mark attended Mike Cohen's Trailside Country School, where he learned to play and sing the simple rhythms of traditional music. His songs, "Spring Lightning and Thunder" and "Susquehanna Down," are on the album "Chesapeake Born" with his father Tom Wisner. Susquehanna Down is a tribute to the simple strength and beauty of the Chesapeake. He commercial fishes for salmon in Prince William Sound, Alaska where he lives with his wife of 22 years, Margarete, and his five children.

Acknowledgments and Donors

Many people and groups have supported the creation of this songbook (including recently and in years past). Special thanks to the following organizations and persons whose support has been invaluable: Joan Clement and The Chesapeake Education, Arts and Research Society (CHEARS), the Center for the Chesapeake Story (CHESTORY), the Calvert Marine Museum (special thanks to Richard Dodds, Robert Hurry, Concetta Lasky), St. Mary's College of Maryland, and Charylu Roberts at O.Ruby Productions.

Special thanks also to the following people who have provided sustained support and guidance to help this songbook see the light of day: Jim Fox, Sara Leeland (Co-founder with Tom of CHESTORY and author of *Gather 'Round Chesapeake*), Mary Ellen and Walter Boynton.

Many people inspired Tom beginning with his own children, Mark, Kirstin, Michael and Karen, and the beloved memory of his deceased daughter Kim, as well as his grandchildren. Special thanks goes to Lois Stewart, who is the "spiritual godmother" of much of Tom's works. Tom felt deep gratitude to the Chesapeake watermen and women who shared their love and knowledge of the Bay with him. Special thanks to the late Dr. L. Eugene Cronin, and also Augie Seckleman, Joseph Mihursky, and Steve Barry and Will Williams and the Arlington Echo staff, Tom Horton, Shari Valerio, Mac Walter, Kathy McCabe, John Cronin, Keith Harancher, Gilbert Byron, and Betty Brady. Thanks also to the thousands of students and teachers Tom worked with throughout the region, who shared their enthusiasm and curiosity with him.

Our gratitude extends also to the many individuals and organizations that have, over time, made financial and other contributions to Tom's work and this songbook. Included among them are:

Avalon Foundation, INC., Sheila Bach, Janet Bartlett, William Bartlett, Phoebe Barth, Don Boecker, Guy Boecker, Donna Boylin, Mary Ellen Boynton, Walter Boynton, Denise Breitburg, Calvert County Cultural Arts Council, the Calverton School—teachers and students, the Eva Cassidy Foundation, the Chesapeake Bay Foundation, the Chesapeake Biological Laboratory, Alice Cronin, Ramona Crowley, John Cumberland, Jared Denhard, Department of Planet Earth, Dudley Family Trust, Melvin Endy, Helen Fornwald, J. N. Fornwald, Alice Fowler, Betty Fowler, C. Bernard Fowler, Frank Fox, Mark Frazer, Chris Fuller, Kathy Glaser, Michael Glaser, Nancy H. Gray, Margo Coffin Goff, Janet Gross, Don Hammett, Jeanne Hammett, Heron Dance, Hollywood Elementary School—teachers and students, Tom Horton, Erik Jannson, Robin Jung, Roy Kahn, Michael King, Sue Kullen, Sara Leeland, Robert Lewis, Carol Locke-Endy, Carol Marcy, Sally Mabelle, The McKnight Foundation, Janie Meneely, Arthur Milholland, Lucille Mostello, Kent Mountford, Nancy K. Mountford, Myrtle Point Park, Jeff Place at the Smithsonian, Doris Poffenberger, Ray Poffenberger, Diane Rausch, Roberta Reeves, Najia Rodes, Christine Schmitthenner, Frank Schwartz, Edward Slunt, Kathleen Slunt, Mark Smith, Nancy Jo Steetle, Talbottown LLC, Meridith Taylor, Ann Trentman, Henry Trentman, the University of Maryland Center for Environmental Science, Kim Walsh, Teresa Whitaker, Will Williams, Margaret Wisner, William Wisner, Diane Wood, Gail Wood, Woodburn Hill Farm. To anyone we might have inadvertently left out: our apologies and many thanks!

Thanks for additional editing to: Jacqueline Gomez, Chris Potts and Linda Zandler.

Final Thoughts

From the Editors

Each of us knew Tom Wisner for many years and worked with him in a wide variety of capacities. Perhaps most important is the deep friendship each of us shared with him for decades. It is our pleasure to share these songs as well as his art and words.

Listed below are some relevant resources and contact information.

Tom's Discography

"Follow on the Water" (2010) and "Made of Water"(2001) are available on line through *CD Baby.com*, *iTunes.com* and other distributional partners.
CDs are also available through *www.chestory.org* and through Finding Home Productions at *www.teresawhitaker.com* or contact *ftzj@cox.net*.
"Chesapeake Born" (1978) and "We've Got to Come Full Circle" (1984) are available through Smithsonian recordings.

Copies of **Singing the Chesapeake** may be purchased from CHESTORY, Finding Home Productions and *www.Amazon.com*.

Photo Credits

Back cover: David Harp • *www.chesapeakephotos.com*
Page 39: Hillary Harp
Page 41: Margo Coffin Groff
Page 43: Karina Glaser

Contacts

CHEARS: Chesapeake Education, Arts and Research Society is a non-profit organization, dedicated to the health of all who share the Chesapeake watershed. *www.chears.org*
CHESTORY is now part of CHEARS. *www.chestory.org*
A virtual archive of Tom Wisner's works is available at: *www.chesapeake-envliteracy.org*
Finding Home Productions: *www.teresawhitaker.com*

Calvert Marine Museum: *www.calvertmarinemuseum.com*
Sara Leeland's book, *Gather 'Round Chesapeake*: *www.saraleelandbooks.net* and *www.Amazon.com*
To view a film on the restoration of Poplar Island which includes Tom's song "All Souls Sing" contact Carlisle Hashim at: *info.greencourses@gmail.com*
Note: Maryland is the first state to have an environmental literacy standard as part of the state's requirements for graduation.

CD tracks:
Male vocals: Tom Wisner on all tracks except track 14, which is Mark Wisner and children
Female vocals: Teresa Whitaker; Male harmonies: Frank Schwartz
Tracks of Tom with children come from a variety of venues over the years.

O.Ruby Productions: *www.orubyproductions.com* and *www.SelfPublishMusicBooks.com*

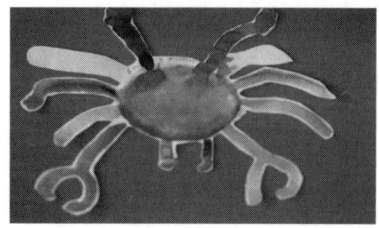